Thy Kingdom Come

ALSO BY RANDALL BALMER

Encyclopedia of Evangelicalism

Religion in American Life: A Short History
(COWRITTEN WITH JON BUTLER AND GRANT WACKER)

Growing Pains: Learning to Love My Father's Faith

Protestantism in America
(COWRITTEN WITH LAUREN F. WINNER)

Religion in Twentieth Century America

Blessed Assurance:
A History of Evangelicalism in America

Grant Us Courage:
Travels along the Mainline of American Protestantism

The Presbyterians
(COWRITTEN WITH JOHN R. FITZMIER)

Mine Eyes Have Seen the Glory:
A Journey into the Evangelical Subculture in America

A Perfect Babel of Confusion:
Dutch Religion and English Culture in the Middle Colonies

Thy Kingdom Come

How the Religious Right Distorts the
Faith and Threatens America

An Evangelical's Lament

RANDALL BALMER

BASIC
BOOKS

A Member of the Perseus Books Group
New York

Books published by Basic Books are available at special discounts for bulk purchases
in the United States by corporations, institutions, and other organizations. For more
information, please contact the Special Markets Department at the Perseus Books
Group, 11 Cambridge Center, Cambridge MA 02142, or call (617) 252-5298 or
(800) 255-1514, or e-mail special.markets@perseusbooks.com.

Interior design by Lisa Kreinbrink

A CIP catalog record for this book is available from the Library of Congress.
10 ISBN 0-465-00519-5
13 ISBN 978-0-465-00519-2
06 07 / 10 9 8 7 6 5 4 3 2 1

For Catharine
and for Christian, Andrew, and Sara

Come, my friends,
'Tis not too late to seek a newer world.
—ALFRED LORD TENNYSON

Contents

Imagine the vanity of thinking your enemy can do you more harm than your enmity.
                                                    —SAINT AUGUSTINE

That cannot be a true religion which needs carnal weapons to uphold it.
                                                    —ROGER WILLIAMS,
                            THE BLOUDY TENET OF PERSECUTION, 1644

Of all the differences between the Old World and the New this is perhaps the most salient: Half the wars of Europe, half the troubles that have vexed European States, from the Monophysite controversies in the Roman Empire of the 5th Century down to the Kulturkamf in the German Empire of the 19th, have arisen from theological differences or from the rival claims of church and state. This whole vast chapter of debate and strife has remained virtually unopened in the United States.
                                                    —JAMES BRYCE, 1893

I do not say our government should be blind to the views of our churches and synagogues. On the contrary, they are responsible organizations entitled to have their views responsibly considered along with the views of others. . . . Whatever different opinions may be held by others, they should feel free to express them without attempting to silence a competing point of view.
                                                    —JOHN F. KENNEDY, 1960

I don't want to see religious bigotry in any form. It would disturb me if there was a wedding between the religious fundamentalists and the political right. The hard right has no interest in religion except to manipulate it.
                                                    —BILLY GRAHAM, PARADE, 1981

And everywhere the good prepare for perpetual war
And let their weapons shape the plan
The way the hammer shapes the hand.
                                                    —JACKSON BROWNE, 2002

Preface

Bullies in the Pulpit

*I'm frankly sick and tired of the political preachers
across this country telling me as a citizen that if I
want to be a moral person, I must believe in "A," "B,"
"C," and "D." Just who do they think they are? And
from where do they presume to claim the right to
dictate their moral beliefs to me?*
— BARRY GOLDWATER, 1964

I WRITE AS A JILTED LOVER. The evangelical faith that nurtured
me as a child and sustains me as an adult has been hijacked by
right-wing zealots who have distorted the gospel of Jesus Christ,
defaulted on the noble legacy of nineteenth-century evangelical
activism, and failed to appreciate the genius of the First Amendment. They appear not to have read the same New Testament that I
open before me every morning at the kitchen counter. When they
do quote the Bible, they wrench passages out of context and offer
pinched, literalistic interpretations—of the Genesis account of creation, for instance—that diminish the scriptures by robbing them
of their larger meaning.

The effect of this right-wing takeover has been a poisoning of
public discourse and a distortion of the faith. Leaders of the Religious Right have managed to persuade many of my fellow evangelical

Christians that it is something akin to sin to vote for anyone who is not a Republican, a perception that the Republican Party has done nothing to discourage. Since its formation in the late 1970s, the Religious Right, a loose federation of politically conservative evangelicals, has become the Republican Party's most reliable constituency, supplying the base of volunteers and voters that organized labor once provided for the Democratic Party.

I have no particular quarrel with that. These politically conservative evangelicals have every right to express themselves in the political arena; the canons of democracy as enshrined in our charter documents, the Declaration of Independence and the Constitution, guarantee that right. But the hard-right stance of the Religious Right represents something less than the best of Christianity, and many of its adherents' positions—on the posting of the Ten Commandments in public places, for example—serve ultimately to diminish the faith. They also serve to alienate evangelical Christians like me, who forever have to explain to incredulous interlocutors that, no, the fact that we love Jesus doesn't mean that we take our marching orders from James Dobson or Karl Rove.

Although the numbers are hard to come by, there are more politically liberal evangelicals than you might think, for one of the great delusions perpetrated by the Religious Right in recent years is that all evangelical Christians are politically conservative. It's probably true—regrettably, in my judgment—that a majority, certainly a plurality, of evangelicals list toward the right politically. But this has not always been so, and even today there is a substantial minority of evangelicals whose understanding of the faith compels them to serve as peacemakers, to take action on behalf of those whom Jesus described as "the least of these," and to champion the rights of women and minorities. Let me put it another way. Am I a feminist? Of course I'm a feminist! I'm a feminist because Jesus was a feminist, and I've chosen to fashion my life, with God's help, after the example of Jesus and his teachings as recorded in the New Testament.

If that makes me a political liberal, then so be it. I claim the word proudly, and I resent equally the hard-right ideologues who have succeeded in turning *liberal* into a term of derision and my fellow liberals who have allowed them to do so. Liberalism in America is responsible for everything from Social Security, civil rights, public education, and equality for women to the very existence of the republic itself. The right of workers to organize against the predatory capitalists of the late nineteenth century, to cite another example, is a *liberal* idea. Liberals believe in tolerance and recognize the beauty of pluralism, although I acknowledge that we ourselves have not always practiced the former perfectly. Like conservatives, liberals have been guilty of excess, but, overall, the tradition of liberalism in America is a distinguished one, and I am pleased to number myself both as an evangelical Christian and as a political liberal.

I'm not alone, although sometimes it feels that way. Other evangelicals have similar views, though we have trouble making our voices heard—at least, we haven't been very skilled at doing so. Part of the problem lies in the fact that, unlike the Religious Right, we don't have radio or television programs, let alone entire media networks. Our views don't lend themselves easily to sloganeering, so we're less likely to show up in the televised shouting matches that pass for political discourse these days. Unlike the Religious Right, we cannot tap into the vast reservoirs of corporate money available to conservative causes.

Some of us have grown increasingly uneasy with the designation *evangelical* because we feel that it has been bastardized by the Religious Right, distorted so completely that it bears scant resemblance to the gospel—the "good news"—of Jesus Christ. I can't tell you how many conversations I've had with disgruntled evangelicals in recent years, evangelicals who believe that the Religious Right has commandeered the faith. Many of them argue passionately that we should find a new term to describe ourselves. On November 3, 2004, the day after the election, I sent a one-word e-mail (a four-letter word) to an evangelical friend in Oregon, a man I've known for more than three decades. He responded sympathetically and told me that he had awakened that morning with something like a hangover—and he hadn't been drinking. He went on to say that, given the pugilistic rhetoric coming from preachers of the Religious Right, he'd resign as an evangelical if he knew where to send the letter.

I understand the impulse to search for a new moniker, but I'm not yet prepared to concede. As an evangelical Christian, someone who takes the Bible seriously and who believes in the transformative power of Jesus, I want to reclaim the faith from the Religious Right. I also want to protest that most of the Religious Right's agenda is misguided, even ruinous, to the nation I love and, ultimately, to the faith I love even more.

Evangelicalism derives its name from *evangel*, a reference to the New Testament and, more particularly, to the first four books of the New Testament, written by the evangelists Matthew, Mark, Luke, and John. In the sixteenth century, Martin Luther, an Augustinian friar, sought to rescue the faith from what he considered the accretions and the abuses of medieval Roman Catholicism. He believed that the Catholic Church had obfuscated the "good news" of the New Testament with a kind of works-righteousness that, in his view, had diminished the Christian notion of grace by inferring that an individual's eternal destiny depended upon how faithfully he attended mass, said confession, went on pilgrimages, or performed other good works. Based on his study of the New Testament, Luther concluded that salvation was bestowed freely by God, regardless of human merit. Luther's "rediscovery of the gospel" led to his excommunication and lent a further, decidedly Protestant, meaning to the term *evangelical*. The ecclesiastical insurgency unleashed by Luther's ideas came to be known as the Protestant Reformation.

Luther diverged from Roman Catholicism over issues of authority. Whereas Rome insisted on twin bases for authority—the Bible and tradition (as interpreted by the Roman Catholic Church)—Luther held that the scriptures alone (*sola scriptura*) provided everything the believer needed to attain salvation. Luther combined this notion of *sola scriptura* with his conviction about the "priesthood of believers," the idea that Jesus himself was high priest. Each individual, then, was accountable for her or his spiritual well-being to God through Jesus, absent the apparatus of the Roman Catholic Church.

Sola scriptura and the priesthood of believers—combined, these two ideas had a revolutionary impact on the Western world. They led, first, to a dramatic rise in literacy as ordinary folks clamored to read and interpret the Bible for themselves and no longer depend upon authoritative pronouncements from the Vatican. Second, the mania for individual interpretation led to a splintering of Protestantism into many and diverse sects, congregations, and denominations, an efflorescence of new faiths that is hardly surprising because the Bible itself admits of many interpretations.

Nowhere was this new energy bred of the Reformation more evident than in the pluralistic environment of North America. Although Luther's reforms were known as *evangelical*—and the Lutheran Church in Germany is still called *Evangelische*—evangelicalism took on particular characteristics in America. Evangelicalism as we know it today emerged from three sources, what I like to call the three P's: Scots-Irish Presbyterianism, Continental Pietism, and the remnants of New England Puritanism. All three came together in the 1730s and 1740s, igniting a huge conflagration of religious enthusiasm known as the Great Awakening. To this day, evangelicalism in America bears the marks of those initial influences—the obsessive introspection of the Puritans, the doctrinal precisionism of the Presbyterians, and the emphasis on a warm-hearted, affective spirituality from Pietism.

American evangelicalism adapted to the trappings of democracy during the decades surrounding the turn of the nineteenth century, as reflected in the populism of the Second Great Awakening, a series of revivals that convulsed three theaters of the new nation: New England, the Cumberland Valley in the South, and upstate New York, an area so frequently singed by revival fires that it became known as the "burned-over district." Evangelicals, principally Methodists and Baptists, "colonized" the frontier regions of the South so thoroughly and effectively that the region bears the unmistakable stamp of evangelicalism to this day. In the North especially, evangelicals took on the task of reforming society according to the standards of godliness. They organized to abolish slavery, to combat the scourge of alcohol abuse, to reform the prison system, to educate women, to create public schools, and generally to make the world a better place.

The reforming zeal flagged somewhat toward the end of the nineteenth century. Faced with urbanization and industrialization, together with the arrival of non-Protestant immigrants, evangelicals began to sense that the larger society had turned against them. The teeming, squalid tenements of lower Manhattan, roiling with labor unrest, no longer resembled the precincts of Zion that evangelicals earlier in the century had hoped to build. Although many evangelicals began to lose hope, their champion in those years was William Jennings Bryan, three-time Democratic nominee for president and Woodrow Wilson's secretary of state. On matters ranging from labor rights and women's suffrage to his opposition to capitalistic monopolies, Bryan, known as the "Great Commoner," would be considered a political liberal by today's standards. His was a *progressive* voice for reform during the decades surrounding the turn of the twentieth century.[1]

In 1925, however, Bryan suffered a brutal character assassination at the hands of H. L. Mencken of the *Baltimore Sun* during the infamous Scopes "monkey trial." The Scopes trial, which took place in Dayton, Tennessee, centered on legal attempts to forbid the teaching of the theory of evolution in the public schools. Bryan had fewer qualms about Darwinism itself than he did about the social effects of evolutionary theory; he worried that Herbert Spencer's social Darwinism or Friedrich Nietzsche's *übermann*, which posited the superiority of some human beings over others, would have disastrous consequences. Such nuances of argument, however, were lost amid the carnival atmosphere of the trial, which unfolded instead as a contest between freedom of scientific inquiry and the superstition of revealed religion.

Although Bryan technically won his case—John Scopes was convicted of violating the Butler Act, which forbade the teaching of evolution—Bryan and his supporters were held up to public ridicule. Evangelicals slumped away from the trial in disgrace and despair, signaling a long retreat into their own subculture of congregations, denominations, Bible camps, Bible institutes, colleges, seminaries, missionary societies, and publishing houses. They remained not so much somnolent as invisible to the larger society until the mid-1970s. Then, a Southern Baptist Sunday school teacher, Jimmy Carter, began to lure evangelicals (Southerners especially) out of their apolitical torpor. Televangelist Pat Robertson, for instance, claimed to have "done everything this side of breaking FCC regulations" to elect Carter in 1976. Four years later, however, Robertson and many other evangelicals abandoned Carter in favor of Ronald Reagan. By then, the Religious Right, this loose federation of politically and religiously conservative organizations that coalesced as a political movement during the Carter administration, had taken on a life of its own.[2]

Leaders of the Religious Right threw their considerable heft behind Reagan in the 1980 election. In so doing, they turned their backs on Carter and also rejected another evangelical, John B. Anderson, Republican congressman from Rockford, Illinois. Anderson was a member of the Evangelical Free Church of America, which happens to be the denomination in which I was reared, and I should add here that I worked for Anderson on Capitol Hill during the summer of 1975; I was a research intern for the House Republican Conference, which he chaired.

The fact that Reagan, as governor of California, had signed a bill legalizing abortion didn't seem to bother the leaders of the Religious Right; nor did the fact that he was divorced and remarried, a circumstance that had disqualified Nelson Rockefeller from any hopes of evangelical support in the 1960s. Although *Newsweek* had pronounced 1976 "The Year of the Evangelical," that declaration turned out to be four years premature; all three major candidates in the 1980 election claimed to be evangelical Christians.

In fairness, not all evangelicals jumped on the Reagan–Religious Right bandwagon. One evangelical publication cautioned that "more space in the Bible is devoted to calls for justice and care for the poor than the fact that human life is sacred." The editorial warned of the dangers of single-issue politics. "Too narrow a front in battling for a moral crusade, or for a truly biblical involvement in politics, could be disastrous," *Christianity Today* concluded. "It could lead to the election of a moron who holds the right view on abortion."[3]

Pollster Louis Field determined that, without evangelical support in the 1980 presidential election, Reagan would have lost to Carter by 1 percent of the popular vote. This is not the place to argue whether Reagan's policies were good or bad, Christian or not Christian, but rapturous leaders of the Religious Right crawled into bed with the Republican Party in 1980 and heralded Reagan's election as a harbinger of the Second Coming. Indeed, Reagan's election in 1980 and his reelection four years later cemented the political alliance between the Religious Right and the Republican Party. Ever since, shamelessly exploiting the "abortion myth," the fiction that the Religious Right mobilized in direct response to the 1973 *Roe v. Wade* decision, leaders of the Religious Right have preached that neoconservative ideology and Republican Party policies offer the most compelling representation of the evangelical faith.

Both theologically and historically, the term *evangelical* has little to do with politics; nor is it in any way incompatible with the great traditions of progressivism in America. Although some students of evangelicalism rely on elaborate theological definitions to describe the movement, I generally offer a functional, three-part definition. First, an evangelical is someone who takes the Bible seriously, even (for many, not all) to the point of literal interpretation. Evangelical literalists, for example, would read the creation stories at the beginning of Genesis in the Hebrew Bible as the actual, historical account of how the world came into being. At the other end of the scriptures, many evangelicals view the book of Revelation as a kind of roadmap for understanding the sequence of events leading to the end of time. Not all evangelicals are so slavishly literal in their approach to the Bible—and, certainly, even those who are practice a selective literalism—but the serious approach to scripture as God's revelation to humanity is one of the hallmarks of evangelicalism.

Second, on the basis of this view of the Bible, evangelicals believe in the importance of conversion as the central criterion for salvation. There are several scriptural bases for this conviction, but the one most often cited appears in the third chapter of the Gospel according to John. There, Nicodemus visits Jesus by night to ask how he can be admitted into the kingdom of heaven. Jesus tells Nicodemus that to gain entry he must be "born again." The phrase recurs in 1 Peter, and evangelicals generally interpret this language to mean that salvation consists of renouncing one's sinfulness—

conversion means "turning toward"—and acknowledging Jesus as savior. For most evangelicals, this conversion is instantaneous, a datable moment, often (though not always) attended by great emotion. A typical evangelical would be able to recount the circumstances surrounding her conversion or "born-again" experience.[4]

Finally, an evangelical is someone who recognizes the imperative to spread the faith, or to *evangelize*. Again, the words of Jesus himself provide the warrant for doing so. "Therefore go and make disciples of all nations," Jesus tells his followers at the end of the Gospel according to Matthew, "baptizing them in the name of the Father and of the Son and of the Holy Spirit, and teaching them to obey everything I have commanded you."[5]

Evangelicalism in America is an extraordinarily diverse movement, encompassing everything from fundamentalists, pentecostals, charismatics, holiness people, followers of the sanctified tradition, Southern Baptists, and several varieties of African American and Hispanic evangelicals. Evangelicalism writ large is the most important social and religious movement in American history; it is America's folk religion. Some polling data suggest that close to half of Americans would fit the definition of *evangelical*.[6]

Before we proceed further, allow me to present my credentials as an evangelical Christian. I was born into an evangelical household while my father was preparing for the ministry at a place called Trinity Seminary and Bible College on the north side of Chicago. He went on to complete his bachelor's degree at the University of Nebraska while serving as an interim pastor in a rural community in the southeastern part of the state, not far from where he was born. His first pastorate was another rural congregation in southern

Minnesota, in the far-distant suburbs of East Chain, a tiny hamlet with a population of about forty-five. In 1963, he took a church in what was for me the booming (and utterly alienating) metropolis of Bay City, Michigan, a blue-collar town of about seventy-five thousand. We moved to Des Moines, Iowa, in 1968, just weeks after my beloved Detroit Tigers, behind the brilliant pitching of Mickey Lolich, upset the St. Louis Cardinals in the World Series. I spent my high school years in Des Moines, fell deeply and irretrievably in love, and headed off to an evangelical college in the fall of 1972.

After graduating from Trinity College in Deerfield, Illinois, I began working as a journalist for its sister institution, Trinity Evangelical Divinity School. Tuition waivers for full-time employees allowed me to earn a degree in church history; my master's thesis on the doctrine of biblical inerrancy, a favorite topic for evangelicals, received some attention and modest acclaim in scholarly circles.

I attended Sunday school during all those years of growing up evangelical—and youth group and church at least twice on Sundays and prayer meeting Wednesday nights. My parents sent me to Bible camp and vacation Bible school in the summers. But faith in Jesus, evangelicals contend, is not a birthright. My parents, like evangelical parents everywhere, expected that I would forge my own "personal relationship with Jesus." One of my earliest memories is of sitting in the kitchen of a rural parsonage in southern Minnesota and asking Jesus into my heart. I was three or four years old when I first renounced my sins and claimed Jesus as my savior. Like many other children of evangelical households, I revisited that moment many times through adolescence—evangelicals call it "rededicating your life to Jesus"—at various junctures of personal or spiritual crisis. I see now that I was repeating that moment of "conversion" time after time because I was trying to get it right and thereby dispel my growing intellectual and existential doubts about the faith.[7]

I distanced myself from evangelicalism during graduate school, not so much as an act of rebellion as an expression of indifference. My graduate work at Princeton revolved around colonial religious history, but it was the televangelist scandals of the mid-1980s, oddly enough, that brought me back to the faith, albeit indirectly. As the scandals surrounding Jim Bakker, Jimmy Swaggart, and Oral Roberts unfolded, I became distressed by the tone of the media coverage. Journalists assumed either that evangelicals were easily duped or that they were the moral equivalent of the televangelists themselves. As a student of American religious history and as someone who had grown up within the evangelical subculture, I knew there was a huge gap between the self-righteous pronouncements of the television preachers and the sincere piety of ordinary evangelicals. I set out to visit various groups of evangelicals at the grass roots—a Bible camp in the Adirondacks, an Indian reservation in the Dakotas, Jesus people in southern California—all in an attempt to reconnect with a more authentic evangelicalism far away from the klieg lights of the televangelists.

I heard a lot of bad sermons in the course of those travels, but I also caught glimpses of the gospel—in the sweet, simple piety of a holiness camp meeting, in the struggle of black evangelicals against racism in the Mississippi Delta, in the dolorous strains of "Seek Ye First the Kingdom of God" or the sublime poetry of "Amazing Grace." "Those small epiphanies affected me," I wrote at the time, "evoking as they did the religion of my childhood." My journey back to the faith was circuitous and, at times, painful, but I came in time to embrace evangelicalism, the good news that Jesus takes our sad, broken lives and somehow, through the miracle of grace, makes us whole.[8]

Although I certainly didn't plan it this way, I have spent a good deal of my career studying evangelicalism. But I am by no means—nor have I ever pretended to be—a detached observer. Evangelical Christianity has shaped me in myriad ways, and it continues to define me in ways that, well over halfway to my allotted threescore and ten, I comprehend only imperfectly. Evangelicalism provides me with an understanding of God and the universe, a system of morality. It also defines my family ties and a circle of friends, many of whom I've had for decades.

Although I identify with evangelicalism, however, I'm not always comfortable with all the trappings of the evangelical subculture. I sometimes designate myself a "lover's-quarrel evangelical" in an effort to distance myself from the narrowness, the legalism, the censoriousness, and the misogyny that too often rears its ugly head among evangelicals. I also want to call evangelicals to their better selves—or, more accurately, to remind them of the teachings of Jesus, as well as the exemplary work of nineteenth-century evangelicals.

That is the task of this book.

My political awakening was no less dramatic or circuitous than my religious awakening. On the morning of October 11, 1972, I persuaded several of my classmates at Trinity College, in the North Shore suburbs of Chicago, to skip chapel that day and accompany me to Wheaton, another suburb thirty-some miles west of Chicago. The speaker at the venerable Edman Chapel at Wheaton College that morning was the junior U.S. senator from South Dakota, George S. McGovern, who was also the Democratic nominee for president. McGovern's father was a Wesleyan Methodist minister in Avon, South Dakota, and the family later moved to Mitchell. While a scholarship student at Dakota Wesleyan University, McGovern won a statewide oratorical contest for a speech entitled "My Brother's Keeper," which argued for the individual's responsibility to all humanity. He interrupted his undergraduate studies to fly combat missions in World War II and returned home as a decorated war hero. After graduation from Dakota Wesleyan, he enrolled as a divinity student at Garrett Evangelical Seminary in Evanston, Illinois, during which time he served as a student pastor in a local Methodist church.

McGovern earned a doctorate from Northwestern University, and after a stint as professor at Dakota Wesleyan, he embarked on a political career—first as executive secretary of the South Dakota Democratic Party and then as a member of Congress and director of President John F. Kennedy's Food for Peace program before his election to the Senate in 1962. During his years in the Senate, McGovern made his mark as an advocate for humanitarian relief and as an opponent of the Vietnam War; with Senator Mark O. Hatfield, Republican of Oregon and an evangelical, he sponsored the "McGovern-Hatfield Amendment to End the War in Vietnam."[9]

Despite his credentials, however, McGovern's appearance at Wheaton had created controversy even prior to his arrival. He had been invited by a student group, but opposition on the part of some of the school's more conservative alumni prompted the college's president, Hudson Armerding, to demand that the invitation be rescinded. Wheaton's most famous alumnus, Billy Graham, had weighed in publicly several weeks earlier with his intention to vote for the incumbent, Richard M. Nixon, Graham's friend going back to their days as anti-Communist crusaders in the 1950s. The students refused to retract the invitation to McGovern, but they agreed to invite Nixon as well. Nixon, however, who was running for reelection from the White House, declined, and by the time my carload of students from Deerfield found a parking place on the leafy streets of Wheaton and shambled to the doors of Edman Chapel, tensions were running high.

I mark that morning in Wheaton as the beginning of my political coming of age as an evangelical Christian. Though I was only seventeen years old, I had been something of a political junkie at least since the 1964 political campaign; my earliest exposure to national affairs had been Kennedy's assassination the previous year. Like other Americans, I knew enough about Nixon to be suspicious— his shameful, methodically slanderous Senate campaign against Helen Gahagan Douglas in 1950, the political slush fund that the *New York Post* had uncovered two years later, the Alger Hiss hearings, the unsuccessful campaigns in 1960 and 1962, and then his remarkable comeback in 1968, abetted by his racially divisive "Southern strategy" and his promise of a "secret plan" to end the war in Vietnam. On June 17, 1972, less than four months before McGovern's appearance at Wheaton, Nixon's Committee to Re-elect the President (known universally by the acronym CREEP) had dispatched undercover operatives to the headquarters of the Democratic National Committee, and despite the White House's best efforts to dismiss the incident as a "third-rate burglary," the signs of political mischief, corruption, and prevarication pointed unmistakably to the Oval Office.

Following an introduction by Tom Skinner, an evangelist and an African American, McGovern tried to address the students. Instead, he was besieged by boos, jeers, and catcalls. Several bands of students paraded around the chapel with huge banners and photographs of Nixon, chanting "four more years!"

I'll confess to a surfeit of naïveté and idealism at the age of seventeen in the fall of 1972, but I was unprepared for the shabby treatment that Wheaton students showered on George McGovern. In time, my shock gave way to rage and finally to genuine curiosity. How could this happen? First, I tried out a bit of shade-tree sociology, reasoning that because the students at Wheaton were more privileged than my classmates and I, maybe they had somehow imbibed reactionary politics—in the club soda, perhaps. But my conversations with students at my decidedly less-affluent campus in Deerfield revealed that they, too, favored Nixon and his conservative politics—to the extent that they harbored any political opinions whatsoever.

My second approach was theological. I do not claim now, nor have I ever claimed, to be a theologian, but it seemed to me, in my commonsense reading of the New Testament, that Jesus had something to say about peacemakers and the poor, and the Hebrew prophets had even more to say about doing justice and walking humbly with God. I detected none of those principles in the platform of the Republican Party in 1972—and certainly not since.

Sociology and theology had both failed me in my attempts to understand why so many evangelicals had embraced Republican ideology, so I turned to history. But as I studied evangelicalism in the nineteenth century, the mystery only deepened as I learned that evangelicals had been in the vanguard of social-reform initiatives for much of the century. Indeed, evangelicalism had animated such movements as the crusade against slavery, temperance reform (a *progressive* movement in the nineteenth century), the female seminary movement, and women's rights. Wheaton College itself had been founded by a Congregationalist minister who was an ardent abolitionist. As I reflected further on nineteenth-century evangelicalism, it occurred to me that in their quest to construct Christ's millennial kingdom here on earth, evangelicals invariably took the part of those on the margins of society, notably slaves and women.[10]

What went wrong? How, I wondered, could evangelicals in the twentieth century have so determinedly forsaken the legacy of their nineteenth-century forebears? When the loose confederation of organizations we know today as the Religious Right began to coalesce late in the 1970s, compounding the betrayal, I grew even more alienated. Their conservative agenda—military expansion, reckless exploitation of the environment, maintenance of racial segregation, and the abolition of the Department of Education—bore scant resemblance to the concerns of nineteenth-century evangelicals.

A word, finally, about terminology. The movement of politically conservative evangelicals that emerged in the late 1970s has been called many things, including the *New Christian Right*, the *Christian Right*, and the *Religious Right*. I prefer the latter, Religious Right, for several reasons.

As with many such designations, the term is more approximate than it is precise. There is no centralized headquarters for "The Religious Right," no computerized listing of card-carrying members. It is purely political shorthand, a term of convenience that, much like the word *generation*, defies easy definition—quick, how many years in a generation? I use the designation *Religious Right* to denote a movement of politically conservative evangelicals who, since the late 1970s, have sought to exert their influence in political, cultural, and legal matters. Some observers call them fundamentalists, although not all fundamentalists are part of the Religious Right, and the Religious Right includes many other kinds of evangelicals—pentecostals, for instance—besides fundamentalists.[11]

The Religious Right, moreover, consists of politically conservative evangelicals both individually and collectively, so it encompasses individual believers as well as a myriad of loosely allied organizations that may or may not fully agree with one another. In its broadest construction, the Religious Right also includes Mormons, some Roman Catholics, and even a few politically and culturally conservative Jews. For the most part, however, the relationship among these groups has been uneasy, a pragmatic marriage born of overlapping interests rather than genuine ardor. While I acknowledge the confluence of interests and some real cooperation in this broader coalition, my focus centers on evangelicals.[12]

The term *New Christian Right* has always baffled me because it suggests there was at one time an *Old* Christian Right. Try as I might as a historian, I've never been able to determine when that was—unless it was the crusty anti-Communism of people like Carl McIntire and Billy James Hargis in the 1940s and 1950s or the stubborn segregationism of the Jim Crow era. Either attribution, I think, demeans the faith.[13]

Christian Right may be less problematic historically, but I find the term objectionable on theological grounds. When I was a child, my mother taught me that whenever anyone asked me about my religion, I should reply, "I don't have a religion; I'm a *Christian.*"

I don't find much that I recognize as *Christian* in the actions and policies of the Religious Right.

Thy Kingdom Come

chapter 1

Strange Bedfellows

The Abortion Myth, Homosexuality, and the Ruse of Selective Literalism

Totalitarianism is easy to administer. Democracy is difficult.... Under totalitarianism it would be a simple matter to regulate and control the morals of the populace; in a democracy morality is best taught in the home and from the pulpit.
—EDITORIAL, SAN JUAN (PUERTO RICO) STAR,
OCTOBER 21, 1960

ON THE FRONT PAGE OF THE MARCH 31, 2005, edition of the *New York Times*, the editors ran an extraordinary photograph well above the fold and directly below the masthead. It showed a group of religious leaders meeting in Jerusalem the previous day: three Islamic muftis, a Sufi sheik, a Roman Catholic prelate, a Greek Orthodox and an Armenian patriarch, the Ashkenazi chief rabbi, and the Sephardic chief rabbi. The purpose of their meeting? A long-overdue interfaith condemnation of religious violence in the Mideast? A call for the Israeli government to forswear the destruction of Palestinian homes in exchange for a pledge to discourage suicide bombers? A resolution against religious bigotry or an entreaty

1

to end the maddening cycle of violence? Perhaps a summit to discuss the war in Iraq? Or the racially, religiously, and politically divisive effects of a huge wall that the Israeli government had been constructing to separate Jews from Palestinians?

No. The religious leaders had gathered in Jerusalem to issue a joint statement of condemnation for a planned gay-pride festival in Jerusalem. They were there at the behest of an evangelical preacher from San Diego, California, named Leo Giovinetti, pastor of Mission Valley Christian Fellowship and a former musician in the casinos of Reno, Lake Tahoe, and Las Vegas. For months, Giovinetti had conducted an online petition drive to urge Israeli politicians to bar the festival. He also worked feverishly behind the scenes to arrange the meeting of religious leaders and to orchestrate its outcome. The clerics did not disappoint. "This is not the homo land," an American spokesman for the gathering declared. "This is the Holy Land." He characterized the proposed festival as "the spiritual rape of the Holy City."[1]

On Wednesday evenings, the Mission Valley Christian Fellowship meets in the sun-dappled sanctuary of a United Methodist church in San Diego. Like most evangelical gatherings these days, the service opened with praise songs, a kind of easy, lilting music that seemed to mesmerize the congregation. The songs were simple and melodically undemanding, the lyrics repetitive and, on the whole, pretty vapid: "O God, awesome in power." "Worship the lamb of God forever." The congregation was dressed California casual: T-shirts, shorts, Hawai'ian shirts. More than a few greying ponytails dotted the audience. When Giovinetti approached the Plexiglas podium, wearing faded denims, boat shoes, and a mint-green oxford shirt that strained to contain his ample waistline, he sounded more like a cheerleader than a traditional parson. "Yeah," he shouted to the congregation. "You sound good tonight!"

It didn't take long for Giovinetti to devolve into his Religious Right persona. After inviting a couple from the congregation to step forward and offer a public testimony—"Manny, would you bring your sweet, little wife up here?"—the pastor declared, "This is a Christian nation. All the leaders at one time were all Christian." The speech that followed was not so much a sermon or a Bible study as a pep talk.

Like a general headed into battle, Giovinetti sought to rally his troops. For several weeks, he had been agitating against the San Diego City Council over the issue of a cross on Mount Soledad, city property. A fixture for fifty years atop one of the tallest hills in the city, the twenty-nine-foot cross had been the subject of several lawsuits. Courts had ruled that such a prominent religious symbol on city land could be construed as an endorsement of one particular faith and, therefore, an infringement of the First Amendment's proscription against religious establishment. The council, faced with a daunting budget crisis and not wanting to defend itself in yet another lawsuit, had voted to turn the Mount Soledad property over to the federal government for use as a veterans' memorial. Giovinetti, however, interpreted the council's action as cowardice, not prudence, and he demanded that the council put the matter before the voters in a referendum.[2]

A front-page article in the *San Diego Union-Tribune* on the morning of my visit to Mission Valley Christian Fellowship gave an account of the six-hour hearing the day before, when Giovinetti had marshaled his forces to demand a referendum rather than cede

Mount Soledad to the federal government. "Emotions ran high for some of the nearly 100 people who spoke in favor of the cross," the article read. "One woman cried, while another called any attempt to remove the cross a 'grotesque perpetuation [*sic*] of a hate crime' against Christians." Giovinetti castigated council members who claimed to be people of faith but voted against retaining the cross. "If you can tell the most high God, sorry, I can't be true to you, then none of us feel confident you're going to be true to us," he said.[3]

At the Mission Valley gathering, Giovinetti exulted in his exploits and those of his followers the day before. "You guys are living out Christianity," he said. "You scare them. You go too far. You scare them because you're not afraid. Don't ever let anyone tell you not to speak up." Giovinetti warmed to his topic. "You must get involved and live your lives in the political arena," he enjoined his audience. Politics even permeated his prayer as he reminded the congregation of his triumph in Israel only six weeks earlier. "Lord, we ask that you will win this battle for the cross," he prayed, "just as you did in the gay-pride matter in Jerusalem."

Although he had ostensibly prepared a meditation on the teachings of Jesus for that evening's gathering of the Mission Valley Christian Fellowship, Giovinetti kept returning to issues of sexuality, which he invariably framed in martial terms. Giovinetti had chosen as the text for study that night Matthew 5, the Sermon on the Mount. "Blessed are the peacemakers," Jesus says, "for they will be called children of God." Giovinetti, however, was eager to set aright those of us who thought we should take Jesus at his word. "People get so confused," Giovinetti began, chuckling derisively. "They actually believe that Jesus was a pacifist." His voice rose in incredulity. "People believe that Jesus is a pacifist!" No, he countered, "there is a battle going on. It is raging."

Giovinetti used the pugilism-not-pacifism theme as a segue back to sexuality, his favorite topic. "I believe that the church is just as intimidated by the homosexual agenda," he thundered, "as Saul and the Israelites were by Goliath." Then, a bit later, he added, "A woman doesn't have a right over her own body. When God said, 'Thou shalt not commit murder,' individual rights went out the window."[4]

Despite the confidence of Giovinetti's declarations, the history of the Religious Right's crusade against abortion is a vexed one. During the 1980s especially, Religious Right activists sought to portray themselves as the "new abolitionists," drawing a parallel between their pro-life agenda and the nineteenth-century campaign against slavery. The Religious Right's attacks on homosexuality represent a reprise of its battle against abortion in decades past. But ever since the Religious Right formulated its position against abortion in the late 1970s and its condemnation of homosexuality in the 1990s, its arguments of opposition have been hampered, at least slightly, by one inconvenient fact: According to the New Testament, Jesus himself said nothing about either abortion or homosexuality, at least nothing that survives in the New Testament accounts.

Why did the Religious Right choose abortion as its defining issue as it consolidated its power in the 1980s? It seems an odd choice, especially for people who pride themselves on biblical literalism, given the paucity of biblical references to the issue. Evangelicals, moreover, have hardly distinguished themselves in the twentieth century as defenders of "the sanctity of life." Many have been, and continue to be, proponents of capital punishment and apologists for various armed conflicts, including the wars in Vietnam and the Persian Gulf and the invasion of Iraq. They have contested this point by drawing a distinction between innocent lives and all others. It's a fair argument, but judging by evangelicals' actions (or lack thereof) over the past half-century, innocent human life terminates at the moment of birth.[5]

For too many evangelicals, the call to defend "the sanctity of life" does not include those lives mired in poverty; nor does it encompass the innocent casualties of war or the African American victims of segregation. The Religious Right has so fetishized the fetus—on the eve of the 1988 Iowa precinct caucuses, a woman told me in hushed tones that the "most dangerous place to be these days is inside a mother's womb"—that they have ignored altogether the travesties of poverty, war, and racism. Innocent human life, for the Religious Right, is clearly a circumscribed category.[6]

Still, the question remains, How did we get to this point? How did leaders of the Religious Right settle on abortion as the issue that would propel them to prominence in the 1980s? Within a couple of years of its formation, the Religious Right had faced a conundrum on matters of sexuality: how to maneuver around the repeated New Testament denunciations of divorce (in part to avoid alienating the growing number of divorced evangelicals) and focus attention instead on what they characterized as other sexual "sins," particularly abortion and homosexuality. This was an especially tricky matter because of evangelicals' professed fidelity to the scriptures as inspired, inerrant, and immutable.

For a people who take pride in a kind of slavish literalism, constructing a case against abortion is not easy. Whereas Roman Catholics rely not only on the Bible for their doctrines, but on the Bible as interpreted by church tradition and "natural law," evangelicals insist on the scriptures alone (*sola scriptura*) as their doctrinal authority. The problem is, the Bible is rather silent on the matter of abortion. Evangelical theologians typically cite passages from the scriptures—Deuteronomy 30:19, Psalm 139:13–16, and Luke 1:41–42—as their biblical warrant for a pro-life position, but other evangelical theologians offer alternate readings of the same texts, interpretations that cast doubt on the antiabortion glosses.

The verse in Deuteronomy, for instance, includes the words "choose life," which some opponents of abortion have made into a bumper sticker. John Goldingay, an evangelical and a professor of Old Testament at Fuller Theological Seminary in Pasadena, California, however, has a different understanding. "It's saying to Israel, choosing life means choosing the way of life, choosing to obey God's word," he said. Psalm 139, to take another example, testifies that "you knit me together in my mother's womb"; pro-life apologists construe that as evidence of God's special care for the fetus, while other evangelicals insist that the passage should be understood as nothing more than a poetic celebration of God's relationship with humanity, especially with ancient Israel. The passage in Luke records simply that "the baby leaped" in Mary's womb, a passage at best inconclusive, although it could probably be used as an argument against late-term abortions. When pressed by a *New York Times* reporter for a clear and unambiguous biblical statement condemning abortion, several pro-life theologians allowed that there were no such passages. "Of course, nothing addresses abortion directly," Willem A. VanGemeren, professor of Old Testament at Trinity Evangelical Divinity School, finally conceded, "but the biblical inference as accepted over the centuries is a witness that cannot be ignored."[7]

The point here is not that the Bible is for or against abortion—I'll leave that argument to the theologians, who seem to be having their share of trouble sorting it out—but that the biblical case against abortion appears to be somewhat less than obvious, less obvious, certainly, than the case against divorce or in favor of those less fortunate, the people Jesus refers to as "the least of these." VanGemeren's ultimate redoubt—"the biblical inference as accepted over the centuries"—is nothing short of fascinating because it represents just the sort of hedging for which evangelicals customarily castigate theological liberals.

The biblical case against divorce, however, is as unambiguous as the arguments against abortion are strained. The prophet Malachi writes, "'I hate divorce,' says the Lord God of Israel, 'and I hate it when people clothe themselves with injustice.'" Jesus, sparring with the Pharisees, declares, "I tell you that anyone who divorces his wife, except for sexual immorality, and marries another woman commits adultery." St. Paul, writing to the Corinthians, says that "a husband must not divorce his wife."[8]

To get from divorce to abortion in the early 1980s, the leaders of the Religious Right resorted to a favorite evangelical redoubt, the ruse of selective literalism. The Religious Right simply ignored or explained away Jesus' admonitions about divorce and focused instead on a political issue that had traction at the time, even though the biblical arguments were weak and, at the very least, contested. Giovinetti in San Diego provides an example of this slick maneuver. Having already declared that God was not a pacifist and was unequivocally opposed to abortion, Giovinetti sought to set his congregation at ease regarding divorce. In the text under discussion in Matthew 5, Jesus says that "anyone who divorces his wife, except for sexual immorality, causes her to become an adulteress, and anyone who marries the divorced woman commits adultery."

Giovinetti's gloss? "That doesn't mean that divorce sometimes isn't a good idea," he said without elaboration. "There are some very good reasons for divorce."[9]

No evangelical seriously argues that divorce isn't bad; nor am I suggesting that evangelicals condone divorce. The issue is one of selective literalism. Most evangelicals worry very little about biblical proscriptions against usury or about Paul's warning that "every woman who prays or prophesies with her head uncovered dishonors her head." Those admonitions, they claim, are culturally determined and therefore dismissible. But those evangelicals who still oppose the ordination of women, on the other hand, choose to interpret Paul's instructions to Timothy literally: "I do not permit a woman to teach or to assume authority over a man; she must be quiet."[10]

The Religious Right takes a similar tack on the matter of divorce. Evangelicals generally, and the Religious Right in particular, chose around 1980 to deemphasize radically the many New Testament denunciations of divorce and to shift their condemnations to abortion and, later, to homosexuality—all the while claiming to remain faithful to the immutable truths of the scriptures. The ruse of selective literalism allowed them to dismiss as culturally determined the New Testament proscriptions against divorce and women with uncovered heads, but they refused to read Paul's apparent condemnations of homosexuality as similarly rooted in—and, arguably, in terms of application, limited to—the historical and social circumstances of the first century.[11]

One way to chart this transition is to look through the pages of *Christianity Today*, the flagship magazine of evangelicalism and the most reliable bellwether of evangelical sentiments, beginning in the 1970s and continuing through the 1980s. Over the course of those years, a remarkable change occurred. During the 1970s, by my count, *Christianity Today* ran eight articles and editorials decrying the growing rate of divorce among evangelicals; by the 1980s, however, after Ronald Reagan's election, those denunciations ceased almost entirely as evangelical condemnations shifted to other, more elusive targets: abortion and, eventually, homosexuality.

Selective literalism continues to serve an important function for the Religious Right. It allows them to locate sin *outside* of the evangelical subculture (or so they think) by designating as especially egregious those dispositions and behaviors, homosexuality and abortion, that they believe characteristic of others, not themselves. This externalization of the enemy is a favorite tactic of fundamentalists everywhere, be they Muslim fundamentalists or the members of the Religious Right, who insist on viewing the world through the lenses of dualism or Manichaeism. They construct strict delineations between right and wrong—careful, of course, to place themselves on the right side of whatever lines they draw. Divorce was too close for comfort—many fellow believers had transgressed this boundary themselves—but abortion was somehow different, something that they could pretend existed only in the secular world they reviled.[12]

My question to the Religious Right is this: If you are serious about your professed commitment to biblical literalism, why are you not working to *outlaw* divorce? Not to make it more difficult to obtain a divorce, but to make it illegal, except in cases of marital infidelity. If you concede—as you must, however grudgingly—that the Bible has little or nothing to say about abortion, and you acknowledge—as you must—that the Bible has relatively more to say about divorce, then how can you countenance divorce (as evangelicals have done, albeit reluctantly) and exert so much energy trying to outlaw abortion?

By their own logic of fidelity to the scriptures, evangelicals should be expending far more energy working to make divorce illegal—not more difficult, mind you, because they are not content simply to make obtaining an abortion more difficult; they want the practice outlawed completely. Why, then, is the Religious Right, which claims allegiance to the scriptures, not working to outlaw divorce?[13]

The answer, I suspect, is that the issue of abortion has served the Religious Right very effectively for more than two decades. Although the Religious Right was slow to pick up on abortion as a political issue, it proved to be a potent one for them during the 1980s, in part because Reagan championed the pro-life cause—despite the fact that as governor of California, he had signed into law a bill legalizing abortion. Reagan kept the antiabortion rhetoric alive throughout his presidency, repeatedly promising an amendment to the Constitution that would outlaw abortion. He never delivered on that promise; nor did his vice president and successor as president, George H. W. Bush, who in 1980 had campaigned against Reagan for his party's presidential nomination as a pro-choice Republican. Although both men coveted the support of the Religious Right, neither made good on his promise to outlaw abortion.

In the 1980s, in order to solidify the shift from divorce to abortion, the Religious Right constructed an *abortion myth*, one accepted by most Americans as true. Simply put, the abortion myth is this: Leaders of the Religious Right would have us believe that their movement began in direct response to the U.S. Supreme Court's 1973 *Roe v. Wade* decision. Politically conservative evangelical leaders were so morally outraged by the ruling that they

instantly shed their apolitical stupor in order to mobilize politically
in defense of the sanctity of life. Most of these leaders did so reluctantly and at great personal sacrifice, risking the obloquy of their
congregants and the contempt of liberals and "secular humanists,"
who were trying their best to ruin America. But these selfless,
courageous leaders of the Religious Right, inspired by the opponents of slavery in the nineteenth century, trudged dutifully into
battle in order to defend those innocent unborn children, newly
endangered by the Supreme Court's misguided *Roe* decision.[14]

It's a compelling story, no question about it. Except for one
thing: It isn't true.

Although various Roman Catholic groups denounced the ruling, and *Christianity Today* complained that the *Roe* decision
"runs counter to the moral teachings of Christianity through the
ages but also to the moral sense of the American people," the vast
majority of evangelical leaders said virtually nothing about it;
many of those who did comment actually applauded the decision.
W. Barry Garrett of *Baptist Press* wrote, "Religious liberty, human
equality and justice are advanced by the Supreme Court abortion
decision." Indeed, even before the *Roe* decision, the messengers
(delegates) to the 1971 Southern Baptist Convention gathering in
St. Louis, Missouri, adopted a resolution that stated, "we call upon
Southern Baptists to work for legislation that will allow the possibility of abortion under such conditions as rape, incest, clear evidence of severe fetal deformity, and carefully ascertained evidence
of the likelihood of damage to the emotional, mental, and physical
health of the mother." W. A. Criswell, former president of the
Southern Baptist Convention and pastor of First Baptist Church
in Dallas, Texas, expressed his satisfaction with the *Roe v. Wade*

ruling. "I have always felt that it was only after a child was born and had a life separate from its mother that it became an individual person," the redoubtable fundamentalist declared, "and it has always, therefore, seemed to me that what is best for the mother and for the future should be allowed."[15]

The Religious Right's self-portrayal as mobilizing in response to the *Roe* decision was so pervasive among evangelicals that few questioned it. But my attendance at an unusual gathering in Washington, D.C., finally alerted me to the abortion myth. In November 1990, for reasons that I still don't entirely understand, I was invited to attend a conference in Washington sponsored by the Ethics and Public Policy Center, a Religious Right organization (though I didn't realize it at the time). I soon found myself in a conference room with a couple of dozen people, including Ralph Reed, then head of the Christian Coalition; Carl F. H. Henry, an evangelical theologian; Tom Minnery of Focus on the Family; Donald Wildmon, head of the American Family Association; Richard Land of the Southern Baptist Convention; and Edward G. Dobson, pastor of an evangelical church in Grand Rapids, Michigan, and formerly one of Jerry Falwell's acolytes at Moral Majority. Paul M. Weyrich, a longtime conservative activist, head of what is now called the Free Congress Foundation, and one of the architects of the Religious Right in the late 1970s, was also there.

In the course of one of the sessions, Weyrich tried to make a point to his Religious Right brethren (no women attended the conference, as I recall). Let's remember, he said animatedly, that the Religious Right did not come together in response to the *Roe* decision. No, Weyrich insisted, what got us going as a political movement was the attempt on the part of the Internal Revenue Service

(IRS) to rescind the tax-exempt status of Bob Jones University because of its racially discriminatory policies.

Bob Jones University was one target of a broader attempt by the federal government to enforce the provisions of the Civil Rights Act of 1964. Several agencies, including the Equal Employment Opportunity Commission, had sought to penalize schools for failure to abide by antisegregation provisions. A court case in 1972, *Green v. Connally*, produced a ruling that any institution that practiced segregation was not, by definition, a charitable institution and, therefore, no longer qualified for tax-exempt standing.

The IRS sought to revoke the tax-exempt status of Bob Jones University in 1975 because the school's regulations forbade interracial dating; African Americans, in fact, had been denied admission altogether until 1971, and it took another four years before unmarried African Americans were allowed to enroll. The university filed suit to retain its tax-exempt status, although that suit would not reach the Supreme Court until 1983 (at which time, the Reagan administration argued in favor of Bob Jones University).

Initially, I found Weyrich's admission jarring. He declared, in effect, that the origins of the Religious Right lay in *Green v. Connally* rather than *Roe v. Wade*. I quickly concluded, however, that his story made a great deal of sense. When I was growing up within the evangelical subculture, there was an unmistakably defensive cast to evangelicalism. I recall many presidents of colleges or Bible institutes coming through our churches to recruit students and to raise money. One of their recurrent themes was, We don't accept federal money, so the government can't tell us how to run our shop—whom to hire or fire or what kind of rules to live by. The IRS attempt to deny tax-exempt status to segregated private schools, then, represented an assault on the evangelical subculture, something that raised an alarm among many evangelical leaders, who mobilized against it.

For his part, Weyrich saw the evangelical discontent over the Bob Jones case as the opening he was looking for to start a new conservative movement using evangelicals as foot soldiers. Although both the *Green* decision of 1972 and the IRS action against Bob Jones University in 1975 predated Jimmy Carter's presidency, Weyrich succeeded in blaming Carter for efforts to revoke the tax-exempt status of segregated Christian schools. He recruited James Dobson and Jerry Falwell to the cause, the latter of whom complained, "In some states it's easier to open a massage parlor than to open a Christian school."[16]

Weyrich, whose conservative activism dates at least as far back as the Barry Goldwater campaign in 1964, had been trying for years to energize evangelical voters over school prayer, abortion, or the proposed equal rights amendment to the Constitution. "I was trying to get those people interested in those issues and I utterly failed," he recalled in an interview in the early 1990s. "What changed their mind was Jimmy Carter's intervention against the Christian schools, trying to deny them tax-exempt status on the basis of so-called de facto segregation."[17]

During the meeting in Washington, D.C., Weyrich went on to characterize the leaders of the Religious Right as reluctant to take up the abortion cause even close to a decade after the *Roe* ruling. "I had discussions with all the leading lights of the movement in the late 1970s and early 1980s, post–*Roe v. Wade*," he said, "and they were all arguing that that decision was one more reason why Christians had to isolate themselves from the rest of the world."[18]

"What caused the movement to surface," Weyrich reiterated, "was the federal government's moves against Christian schools." The IRS threat against segregated schools, he said, "enraged the Christian community." That, not abortion, according to Weyrich, was what galvanized politically conservative evangelicals into the Religious Right and goaded them into action. "It was not the other things," he said.[19]

Ed Dobson, Falwell's erstwhile associate, corroborated Weyrich's account during the ensuing discussion. "The Religious New Right did not start because of a concern about abortion," Dobson said. "I sat in the non-smoke-filled back room with the Moral Majority, and I frankly do not remember abortion ever being mentioned as a reason why we ought to do something."[20]

During the following break in the conference proceedings, I cornered Weyrich to make sure I had heard him correctly. He was adamant that, yes, the 1975 action by the IRS against Bob Jones University was responsible for the genesis of the Religious Right in the late 1970s. What about abortion? After mobilizing to defend Bob Jones University and its racially discriminatory policies, Weyrich said, these evangelical leaders held a conference call to discuss strategy. He recalled that someone suggested that they had the makings of a broader political movement—something that Weyrich had been pushing for all along—and asked what other issues they might address. Several callers made suggestions, and then, according to Weyrich, a voice on the end of one of the lines said, "How about abortion?" And that is how abortion was cobbled into the political agenda of the Religious Right.[21]

The abortion myth serves as a convenient fiction because it suggests noble and altruistic motives behind the formation of the Religious Right. But it is highly disingenuous and renders absurd the argument of the leaders of the Religious Right that, in defending the rights of the unborn, they are the "new abolitionists." The Religious Right arose as a political movement for the purpose, effectively, of defending racial discrimination at Bob Jones University and at other segregated schools. Whereas evangelical abolitionists of the nineteenth century sought freedom for African Americans, the Religious Right of the late twentieth century organized to perpetuate racial discrimination. Sadly, the Religious Right has no legitimate claim to the mantle of the abolitionist crusaders of the nineteenth century. White evangelicals were conspicuous by their absence in the civil rights movement of the 1950s and 1960s. Where were Pat Robertson and Jerry Falwell and Billy Graham on August 28, 1963, during the March on Washington, or on Sunday, March 7, 1965, when Martin Luther King Jr. and religious leaders from other traditions linked arms on the march from Selma to Montgomery, Alabama, to stare down the ugly face of racism?

Falwell and others who eventually became leaders of the Religious Right, in fact, explicitly condemned the civil rights movement. "Believing the Bible as I do," Falwell proclaimed in 1965, "I would find it impossible to stop preaching the pure saving gospel of Jesus Christ, and begin doing anything else—including fighting Communism, or participating in civil-rights reforms." This makes all the more outrageous the occasional attempts by leaders of the Religious Right to portray themselves as the "new abolitionists" in an effort to link their campaign against abortion to the nineteenth-century crusade against slavery.[22]

What about the substance of the Religious Right's argument against abortion? Is there a moral equivalence between slavery and abortion? Put another way, would the opponents of slavery in the antebellum period be marching against the *Roe* decision at the turn of the twenty-first century? There is no way to know the answer to that question, of course, but it seems likely that the moral crusaders of the early nineteenth century would indeed be troubled by the widespread incidence of abortion. Still, there are crucial differences between the two issues. Regrettable though it may be, the act of abortion is personal and episodic, whereas slavery was systemic and institutionalized. Another difference: The outlawing of slavery eventually ended that practice, while even the leaders of the Religious Right concede that making abortion illegal will not stop abortion itself.

Charles Colson, one of the Watergate felons who converted to evangelical Christianity and now ranks as one of the foremost apologists for the Religious Right, acknowledges that overturning the *Roe* decision would not make for fewer abortions, at least not in the short term. Colson, who counts himself pro-life, points out that "changing the law is an empty victory unless we also change the moral consensus." James Davison Hunter, a sociologist with ties to the Religious Right, advocates precisely the reverse approach from Colson's. He argues that "while it is appropriate to pursue a legal strategy giving priority to the modification of *Roe v. Wade*, it is not enough to change the law." He adds, "Laws require legitimacy and, therefore, a grass-roots strategy is necessary as well—a changing of hearts and minds."[23]

One of the truly unfortunate developments around the abortion issue over the past several decades is that what passes for debate on the matter has devolved into a bumper sticker war: pro-choice *versus* pro-life, antiabortion *versus* antichoice. The issue is much more complex than that. I think it's appropriate to draw a distinction between abortion as a *moral* issue and abortion as a *legal* issue. Regarding the former, the rights of individual privacy, solidly based in legal precedent and articulated in the Supreme Court's 1965 *Griswold* decision, together with constitutional protections against unreasonable search and seizure, preclude a legal ban on abortion. Besides, despite the pro-life efforts to bestow a kind of fetal citizenship, the state still issues—and has always issued—a certificate at *birth*, not at conception. I happen to be a libertarian on this point: The government should have no jurisdiction whatsoever over gestation—a position, by the way, much more consistent with the Republican Party's avowed principle of less governmental interference in the lives of individuals.[24]

Having affirmed the importance of choice on the basis of personal privacy and liberty, I believe just as fervently that abortion itself is lamentable. Abortion is a fearsome choice with moral repercussions. But it is a choice properly made by the individual and her conscience, not by the state.

This, by the way, is roughly the position of the attorney who argued for the plaintiff in the *Roe* case. Linda N. Coffee, a Southern Baptist, commented after the decision that "legal personhood is separate entirely from a moral or religious view of personhood." Coffee, a member of Park Cities Baptist Church in Dallas, added, "from my personal perspective as a Christian, it would tear me up to have to make a decision on abortion except in the early stages." She concluded, "The Supreme Court decision does not absolve anyone of individual moral or religious responsibility."[25]

The real question for the Religious Right and the Republican Party is how serious they are about reducing (and even eliminating) abortion itself, especially when everyone acknowledges that legal sanctions will not work. Wouldn't the energies of the Religious Right be more productively directed toward campaigns to encourage abstinence, contraception, and adoption, similar to campaigns directed against smoking or alcohol and spousal abuse? Even better, the Religious Right might want to consider the links between abortion rates and the availability of contraception or the economic plight of mothers-to-be facing medical and child-care costs. Surely such initiatives would do more than a legal ban to make abortion rare and unthinkable. The Religious Right might also want to consider the fact that by the time Bill Clinton, a defender of reproductive choice, left office, the abortion rate had fallen to its lowest level since 1974, a year after the *Roe* decision.[26]

Curiously, although the leaders of the Religious Right have been advocating a legal ban on abortion at least since 1980, they have been remarkably silent about the details of their proposals. Will gynecologists be required to report every fertilized egg implanted in the uterus to some government registry so that each pregnancy can be monitored? Which agency would be responsible for such oversight—the Federal Bureau of Investigation or some new entity? (Given the Religious Right's professed aversion to government, the latter option seems unlikely.) Will the government require that a law-enforcement official be present at every obstetrics examination, or merely somewhere on the premises? Will it be a federal, state, or local official? What about miscarriages? How will officials determine whether or not a miscarriage occurred naturally?

For the most part, the Religious Right has not specified sanctions. Senator Tom Coburn of Oklahoma, a physician and an evangelical, has called for capital punishment for any doctor performing an abortion, but that seems a tad harsh. Life in prison, or some lesser sentence? And what about the mother? Shouldn't she face incarceration? So far, leaders of the Religious Right have been divided over whether to provide exceptions in cases of incest or rape, with some insisting that every fetus, regardless of provenance, be brought to term. If such exceptions were allowed, what criteria would have to be satisfied? Surely, the Religious Right would require evidence to corroborate the mother's testimony.

The leaders of the Religious Right have had more than a quarter of a century now to formulate their proposals, but they have failed so far to make public the specifics of their plan. Sometimes the devil, as the saying goes, is in the details.

I agree with the Religious Right that abortion itself is a travesty. But I also agree with the Religious Right that making it illegal will not bring about any appreciable difference in the incidence of abortion. In order to reduce, or even to eliminate, abortion, there must be a shift in the moral climate surrounding the issue. Threats of governmental intrusion into the lives of women, I suspect, simply engender resistance to the antiabortion cause.

My party, the Democratic Party, has utterly botched the abortion issue, I'll not deny that. In their efforts to assert the importance of women's rights and prerogatives, many Democrats have elevated abortion to an intrinsic entitlement and, in so doing, have refused to acknowledge the moral implications of abortion itself. This imperious position has alienated key constituencies once associated with the Democratic Party, especially Roman Catholics. It has also functioned to marginalize many evangelical voters in the Democratic Party—on that issue alone. When I was writing about the grassroots politicking by the Religious Right during the weeks leading up to the Iowa precinct caucuses in 1988, for example, one activist asked me, in all seriousness, how I could consider myself a Christian and still identify myself as a Democrat. At the time, I found the question both humorous and more than a little insulting, but I have encountered that sentiment many times since.

David Warnick, pastor of New Life Community Church in Rathdrum, Idaho, is one example of the dangers the Democratic Party faces due to its strident position on abortion. When I interviewed him in his church office near Coeur d'Alene, he was wearing a red plastic band around his right wrist as a reminder, he said, "to pray about abortion." Although he volunteered that the Democratic Party might more nearly embody Jesus' attitude toward the poor, Warnick insisted that "abortion is the defining issue." He conceded, however, that it wasn't always so. In 1972, Warnick managed the campaign of a pro-choice Republican candidate for the Idaho legislature. Warnick became student body president at the University of Idaho and head of the College Republicans statewide. He worked on Newt Gingrich's initial campaign for Congress in 1978 and later became Gingrich's chief of staff. By then, Warnick had become an implacable foe of legalized abortion. When I asked if he was similarly opposed to capital punishment on the grounds of defending the sanctity of life, Warnick said that he had "no problem" with capital punishment.[27]

In order for the Democratic Party to have any chance of reclaiming disaffected evangelical voters, it must rearticulate its position on abortion by drawing a clear distinction between the *legal* and the *moral* considerations surrounding the issue. The notion that abortion should be legal but unthinkable runs the risk of alienating the far-left factions of the Democratic Party, but it is worth remembering that the only two successful Democratic candidates for president since the *Roe* decision held similar views. In 1976 Jimmy Carter declared that, although he was "personally opposed" to abortion, he did not want to make it illegal. Despite enormous pressure from the Catholic bishops toward the close of his campaign, Carter held his ground. Bill Clinton frequently said that he wanted abortion to be "safe, legal, and rare."[28]

Leaders of the Republican Party show no signs of wanting to alter the status quo. And why should they? Am I the only person in America who finds it curious that even though the Republican–Religious Right coalition seized control of the House of Representatives in 1995, the presidency in 2001, and the Senate in 2003, these conservatives have made no serious attempt to outlaw abortion, their stated goal? Republicans recognize that their putative pro-life stance coupled with the Democratic Party's obdurate refusal to distinguish between the legal and the moral arguments surrounding abortion works very much to their advantage. It energizes single-issue voters and ensures that the Republican base turns out to the polls, even though many Republicans, like Warnick in Idaho, concede that the Democratic agenda overall, especially its attitudes toward the poor, more nearly reflects the teachings of Jesus. Democrats, for their part, can't do the math. How any major party can go into an election campaign prepared to concede close to 50 percent of the electorate—the majority of evangelicals combined with conservative Roman Catholics—before a single ballot is cast staggers the imagination.[29]

The abortion debate has festered for decades now, with no appreciable movement on either side and no resolution in sight. Liberals trumpet individual liberties and legal rights but slough off the issues of individual responsibility by refusing to acknowledge the tragedy of abortion itself. Leaders of the Religious Right, despite their putative aversion to governmental interference in individuals' lives, have chosen to focus their energies on legal redress rather than work to alter the moral climate that would diminish the demand for abortion. The abolitionists whom the leaders of the Religious Right claim as their inspiration did precisely the opposite. They succeeded first in forging a moral consensus against the abomination of slavery. The force of that consensus ultimately brought about legal change, albeit at great cost to the republic.

The election of Bill Clinton stalled the Religious Right's progress on the abortion issue—under no circumstances would Clinton either sign legislation limiting a woman's right to choose or nominate a pro-life justice to the Supreme Court. Clinton's election in 1992 and his reelection in 1996 halted, at least temporarily, the advance of the Religious Right, which is the principal reason its adherents reviled him so vigorously and sought so determinedly to drive him from office. Clinton's presence in the Oval Office also meant that the antiabortion cause would founder in the 1990s. If the pro-life forces couldn't outlaw abortion during the dozen years of the Reagan and Bush administrations, how could the Religious Right call its constituency to the ramparts during the Clinton administration? Religious Right fundraisers also discovered that they could no longer count on stoking antiabortion sentiments to raise funds, so they needed another issue to energize their base. Complicating their quandary further, after the fall of the Soviet Union, they couldn't revert to the menace of Communism.

The Religious Right desperately searched for a new enemy. The so-called secular humanists were always handy, but in a nation where at least 90 percent of Americans profess to believe in God or a supreme being, the argument that the United States was becoming irreligious was wearing thin. In an era of massive trade deficits by the end of the first Bush administration, the Japanese and the Saudis looked a bit sinister, but we drove automobiles produced by the former and slurped the oil of the latter.

After casting about, the Religious Right came up with a new foil, an enemy right here among us: homosexuals. Although evangelicals have always been uneasy about homosexuality, gays and lesbians suddenly represented all manner of threats. They were corrupting our children and infecting our military. Bill Clinton's commitment to civil rights protections for homosexuals and his "don't ask, don't tell" policy for the armed forces served to fuel those suspicions.

James Dobson, head of Focus on the Family, and Bill McCartney, founder of Promise Keepers, campaigned tirelessly in 1992 for the passage of Amendment 2 in Colorado, which banned "all legislative, executive, or judicial action at any level of state or local government designed to protect the status of persons based on their 'homosexual, lesbian or bisexual orientation, conduct, practices or relationship.'" The referendum passed, although it was struck down as unconstitutional four years later by the U.S. Supreme Court. Still, leaders of the Religious Right continued to excoriate what they called the "gay lifestyle" and the "gay agenda." The former term, gay lifestyle, was coded language; it asserted that same-sex attraction was volitional, that gays and lesbians had chosen their way of life, an assertion at best unproven and generally refuted by medical and scientific evidence.[30]

When the state of Hawai'i made provisions for homosexual couples to be "reciprocal beneficiaries" and the state of Vermont legalized civil unions in 2000, the Religious Right seized on the issue with a vengeance. I won't dispute that the leaders of the Religious Right were acting, at some level, out of conviction, but they, along with leaders of the Republican Party, sensed a political opportunity as well. And when the Massachusetts Supreme Court cleared the way for same-sex marriage in 2003 conservatives sensed—correctly, as it turned out—that they had a potent political issue that they could turn to their advantage. By accident or by design (I suspect the latter), referenda banning same-sex marriages appeared on the ballot in key states during the 2004 election, an action that virtually assured a higher turnout from conservative voters opposed to same-sex unions.

Why has homosexuality proven to be such a durable issue for the Religious Right? Like abortion, it allows evangelicals to externalize the enemy, based on the supposition that no true believer could be gay or lesbian. It also works because it plays on popular anxieties about sexual identity and gender roles in the wake of the women's movement of the 1960s. "We would not be having the present moral crisis regarding the homosexual movement if men and women accepted their proper roles as designated by God," Jerry Falwell wrote back in 1980.[31]

The Religious Right also recognizes that anxieties over sexuality work to their advantage in arenas other than politics, or at least politics narrowly construed. For two days in May 2005, I attended a strategy session for a group called the Association for Church Renewal. The group met in a Holiday Inn conference room in Alexandria, Virginia, just across the Potomac River from Washington. The gathering provides a kind of microcosm for understanding the so-called culture wars. "Something is terribly, definitely wrong in the church," Gerald Walz, a representative of the Institute on Religion and Democracy, a Religious Right organization, told those in attendance. "We want to transform not only our church, but our culture."

Founded in 1996, the Association for Church Renewal is a federation of approximately thirty evangelical "renewal groups" within mainline (generally liberal) Protestant denominations. The association, which functions with the assistance of the Institute on Religion and Democracy, has identified what it considers the contested issues within mainline Protestant denominations: "orthodox faith, holy living, moral relativism, marriage and family, human sexuality, neo-pagan worship, God-language, the free exercise of religion at home and abroad, the sanctity of life, and world mission and evangelism." The outcome of denominational discussions of these matters, the people associated with the organization contend, is crucial for the future of the denominations and, by extension, Christianity itself.

The meeting, spread over a day and a half, consisted almost entirely of reports from the leaders of the various renewal organizations, many of whom consider their groups, as one leader described it, "a church within a church." They see themselves as the remnant of the faithful in an ecclesiastical context that has succumbed to liberalism. The informal presentations included a lot of jabs at liberals generally, but their particular target was denominational leadership, which, according to the participants, lists decidedly to the left, especially on matters of sexuality. One man offered a caricature of the thinking of theologically liberal denominational leaders: "Let's rewrite the Bible the way that God would have written the Bible if he'd known as much as we do."

What has been the effect of the drift toward theological liberalism in mainline denominations? In the United Church of Christ, according to David Runnion-Bareford of Biblical Witness Fellowship, the denomination has shrunk from eighty-five hundred congregations in 1957 to fifty-eight hundred. The United Methodists in the room claimed that the hemorrhaging in their denomination was even more dramatic, the equivalent of one congregation of two hundred fifty people per day for the past twenty-eight years. "The crisis facing the Presbyterian Church is real," one man warned. Another conferee asserted that the congregations "that are preaching socialism rather than the gospel are dying." Another noted, in a mixed metaphor, that evangelicals are "swimming upstream in a denomination that has a masochistic death wish."

The collective focus of consternation there in Alexandria was what one participant called "the homosexual issue," especially same-sex unions and the ordination of lesbians and gays. The elevation of V. Gene Robinson, an openly gay man, as the Episcopal bishop of New Hampshire in 2003 sharpened the issue, especially for Episcopalians, but the representatives seated around the conference table told of similar outrages in their respective denominations.

Issues surrounding homosexuality have emerged as a kind of litmus test for these evangelicals. For those gathered in Alexandria, there was no biblical ambiguity regarding homosexuality. "Is the church of Jesus Christ going to condone those things in us that Jesus died to redeem?" one participant asked rhetorically. He went on to affirm that the twin evils of gay ordination and gay marriage represented "a hill to die on."

Voice after voice rose to report struggles against those within a denomination who would sanction homosexuality and same-sex unions. "This is a deception that is demonic in nature," the head of Missions Renewal Network declared, referring to his denomination's tolerance of gays and lesbians. "They are evil," Karen Booth, a representative of a group called Transforming Congregations, said about those who take a liberal stand on the issue. "They are evil people, and they need to be confronted." Everyone agreed that attitudes toward homosexuality constituted the line of demarcation between conservative and liberal, orthodox and something somehow less than Christian. "We're in a culture war in this country," one man said. "We need to proclaim the gospel."

For a day and a half, I heard about little else than sex; indeed, the conversation sounded at times almost salacious. Toward the end of the gathering, I did something that I've rarely done in two decades of writing about evangelicals. Though I was there as a reporter and an observer, I couldn't help asking a question. The question arose from a growing frustration with the group's selective literalism—they alone (and those who agreed with them) seemed to understand the mind of God.

So, with some trepidation and with prefatory apologies for intruding into the conversation, I posed my question: How many people in the room had a theological objection to the ordination of women? The participants clearly were confused by the query. They looked at one another and around the conference table, then back at me to determine, I suppose, whether or not it was a serious question. Finally, one person out of twenty (an Episcopal woman) raised her hand and affirmed that she opposed women's ordination. Why do you ask, they wanted to know. I replied that, as a historian, I was fairly certain that if this group had been meeting twenty or thirty years earlier, they would be strategizing about how to stop the ordination of women, and they would be quoting scripture to justify their position.

The room fell silent for a moment. They asked what I was getting at.

I argued for the possibility of historical contingency on some of these issues, that what seems clear and unequivocal today might be the product less of unalloyed fidelity to the Bible than of the prevailing prejudices of the culture. Divorce, for instance, was excoriated by evangelicals with near unanimity in the 1950s, 1960s, and 1970s, and the arguments were buttressed with a flurry of proof-texts, but evangelicals are conspicuously mute about the issue now.

Again, the room was silent. With more bluster than judgment, I forged ahead. I guess what worries me, I continued, is that if I had been alive 160 years ago or 60 years ago, and the issues of the day were, respectively, slavery and segregation—I worry that I might have been one of those people *quoting scripture* in defense of slavery and segregation. The social location of these issues, I suggested, gave me pause about adding my voice to their blanket denunciations of homosexuality, especially when Jesus himself said nothing about the matter.

Silence again. "Well, this is different," someone said.

Okay, I replied, eager to be instructed on the matter. How is it different?

A long pause. "It's just different."

After another awkward silence, the moderator suggested we move on to the next report.

Despite all of the complaints about the direction of mainline denominations, most of the conferees in Alexandria remained confi-

dent. They believed that by using the "wedge" issues of gay ordination and same-sex unions, they would ultimately prevail in the
ideological battles within their denominations. At times, the tone
verged on triumphalism. "The liberals are losing," the leader of
United Methodist Action said, with a touch of sarcasm in his voice,
"so they are starting to talk about unity." The moderator cited the
overwhelming number of evangelicals in Methodist seminaries, a
circumstance, he said, that augured well for the future of the denomination. "We have reason to be greatly encouraged," he said.
"I've read the end of the book," one man declared, referring to the
Bible, "and I know that we win." Someone else spoke about offering liberals "a gracious exit" from the church, allowing them to retain their pensions in exchange for ceding the denomination to the
conservatives. "The battles may go on," another said, "but the war
is won."

As a student of American religious history, I'd be hard pressed to
dispute the conferees' assessment of the state of mainline Protestantism. Like the Democratic Party, and for many of the same reasons, mainline Protestantism is virtually moribund at the turn of the
twenty-first century. The reasons for its demise, however, should
provide a cautionary tale to evangelicals in their quest for political
and cultural influence. In the years following World War II, mainline Protestants—Presbyterians, Methodists, Congregationalists,
Episcopalians, Lutherans, and northern Baptists—plunged headlong into a movement called ecumenism, which sought to elide theological differences in the name of Christian unity.[32]

Protestant ecumenism in the 1950s was in part a cold war
construct; we Americans felt that we had to show the world, particularly the Communists, that America was a godly nation. In the rush

toward religious and theological consensus, however, mainline Protestantism aligned itself more-or-less uncritically with white, middle-class American culture in the 1950s and early 1960s. This fusion was nicely symbolized by Dwight Eisenhower's laying the cornerstone for the Interchurch Center in upper Manhattan on October 12, 1958. The presence of the president of the United States at this event lent a kind of legitimacy to mainline Protestantism and provided at least a veneer of validation to its attempts to embody American, patriotic values. This was the era when "under God" was inserted into the Pledge of Allegiance and "In God We Trust" was emblazoned on our currency. But the lessons of American history and the example of mainline Protestantism teach us that religious fervor and conviction function best on the margins of society and not in the councils of power and influence. One reading of the demise of mainline Protestantism, then, is that it sought to ally itself too closely with middle-class values and the pursuit of cultural respectability in the 1950s; in the process, it lost its prophetic edge.[33]

Is the Religious Right doing the same with its close alliance to the Republican Party and its lust for political power and cultural influence? The elaborate construction and propagation of the abortion myth, together with the ruse of selective literalism, which diverted evangelicals from their birthright of fidelity to the Bible, suggests the perils of pandering for power. What should we read into the fact that evangelical conservatives dropped their longstanding denunciations of divorce about the same time they embraced Ronald Reagan, a divorced and remarried man, as their political savior in 1980? Not only have leaders of the Religious Right betrayed scripture, but they have shamelessly manipulated important issues—gay rights, abortion—for partisan purposes, all the while ignoring Jesus' teachings on other matters. Deeply complicated subjects have become mere political cudgels in the hands of the Religious Right, issues calculated to rally the faithful for political ends. They have taken complex, human problems and reduced them to campaign slogans. They have distorted the faith, the "good news" of the New Testament, into something ugly and punitive.[34]

The lesson of both mainline Protestantism in the 1950s and the Religious Right in the 1980s and beyond is that religion functions best when it is not tethered to particular political parties or ideologies. Religion works best when it operates from the margins of society and not at the centers of power and when it remains true to the faith and refuses to allow political interests to shape—or commandeer—its doctrines.

But the reverse is also true: Political movements and politicians who seek to cloak themselves in the mantle of religious legitimacy invariably fall prey to self-righteousness, intolerance, and fanaticism. American history is littered with examples, from the anti-Masonic movements of the antebellum period and the nativism of the Know-Nothing Party to the "family values" ideology of the second Ku Klux Klan and the anti-Communism of the McCarthy era. Like the Religious Right in the twenty-first century, the Puritans of the seventeenth century detested the idea of separating church and state almost as much as they abhorred the notion of toleration. Quakers and others paid with their lives for challenging a political order that had wrapped itself in religious authority.

The abortion myth and the ritual castigation of homosexuals have paid off handsomely for the Religious Right by providing them a political platform. But at what price? The political calculus behind choosing the issues of abortion and homosexuality while ignoring other issues, such as care for the poor and opposition to war, to name only two, exposes the evangelical ruse of selective literalism, which leads both to a distortion of the gospel and to a kind of mechanistic reading of the scriptures that takes no account of historical contingency.

I'm in no position to instruct Leo Giovinetti on how to preach to his congregation in San Diego, and I'm confident that he would refuse to listen even if I tried. I wonder, though, what would happen if, instead of offering tortured explanations about how Jesus favored war over peace or reveling in having thwarted a gay-pride event in Jerusalem, Giovinetti talked once in a while about what Jesus himself declared was the heart of the gospel. "Love the Lord your God with all your heart and with all your soul and with all your mind," Jesus said, adding, "Love your neighbor as yourself." Giovinetti styles himself as a kind of righteous provocateur, grandstanding in front of the city council or jetting halfway across the world to cadge headlines for his condemnation of homosexuals. But I know of no concept more radical than Jesus' declaration of love.[35]

This radical notion of love doesn't comport very well with most political agendas. Politics and politicians concern themselves with the acquisition and the exercise of power, whereas the ethic of love, more often than not, entails vulnerability and the abnegation of power. For the Religious Right, the quest for power and political influence has led to both distortions and contortions—the perpetration of the abortion myth, for instance, or the selective literalism that targets certain sexual behaviors for condemnation, while ignoring others. History, moreover, teaches us the dangers of allying religion too closely with politics. It leads to intolerance in the political arena, and it ultimately compromises the integrity of the faith.

chapter 2

Where Have All the Baptists Gone?

Roy's Rock, Roger Williams, and the First Amendment

As religion must always be a matter between God and individuals, no man can be made a member of a truly religious society by force or without his own consent, neither can any corporation that is not a religious society have a just right to govern in religious affairs.
—ISAAC BACKUS, 1781

SOME OF THE THINGS I LEARNED FROM the radio while traveling the two hundred miles from George Bush Intercontinental Airport in Houston to Longview, Texas:

- The intellectual and scientific case for evolution is crumbling.
- Global warming is a myth.
- The flat income tax is a superb idea.
- "Satan wants the United States to be kind to pluralism."
- The reason we swear an oath on the Bible is because the Bible was the sole foundation of American law.
- The world has an unlimited supply of oil.

- The Constitution provides no guarantee of personal privacy.
- Government fuel-efficiency standards kill people.
- Satan dominates the secular media.

My visit to East Texas came at a strange time. A day earlier, Pat Robertson had issued his *fatwa* against the president of Venezuela, and I was certain, given their hysteria over terrorism, that my friends on the Religious Right would join me in calling for Robertson's detention and interrogation on suspicion of making a terrorist threat. (The televangelist is no stranger to making death threats, of course, though in the past he has generally targeted Supreme Court justices, not foreign heads of state.) The only real question, it seemed to me, was whether we should handle Robertson's interrogation domestically, entrust him to the professionals at Guantánamo Bay, or risk the possibility of torture by turning the televangelist over to what the Bush administration euphemistically calls "extraordinary rendition," or questioning by friendly third countries that are not averse to such measures.[1]

But Robertson's statement elicited nary a comment from what passes for Christian radio in East Texas, although one pundit allowed that the televangelist might try to convert the Venezuelan president before calling for his assassination.

I learned something else in the course of my travels through the triple-digit heat of a Texas summer: There seems to be at least some truth in the oft-quoted statement of Bill Moyers (the pride of Marshall, Texas) that in East Texas there are more Baptists than there are people. I passed First Baptist Church and Second Baptist Church, Long Range Baptist Church, Faith Family Baptist Church, Charity Baptist Church, Timpson Missionary Baptist Church, Appleby

Baptist Church, Holly Springs Baptist Church, First Freewill Baptist Church, Zion Hill Baptist Church, Friendship Baptist Church, Friendship Bobo Baptist Church, Heritage Baptist Church, Pleasant Hill Baptist Church, Pleasant Valley Baptist Church, and Grace Baptist Church, which, according to a large sign, featured "Old Fashion Preaching"—to name only a few.

Given all of these churches, given all of these angry voices defending the faith on my car radio, imagine my surprise that evening when I attended a huge Religious Right rally at the Maude Cobb Convention and Activity Center in Longview and learned that, despite all appearances to the contrary, East Texas is actually in the grip of Satan.

For months, Rick Scarborough, a preacher and head of an organization called Vision America, had been promoting his "Enough Is Enough!" rally in Longview. He promised his audience appearances by Louie Gohmert, U.S. Congressman from East Texas, and Roy Moore, former chief justice of the Alabama Supreme Court, better known as the "Ten Commandments Judge." Several thousand East Texans arrived for the rally, many of them toting their Bibles, eager to hear the famous judge. "I've had this on my calendar for months," one woman shrieked to an acquaintance in the lobby of the convention center. A deep bass voice on a recorded musical sound track sang, "Something is wrong with America" in ominous tones, but the song concluded triumphantly, "The army of God is taking America back!"[2]

As the foot soldiers of the Almighty took their seats, a trio of singers entertained them—one of the songs featured a "blood-stained Bible"—and then asked the congregation to stand for the singing of "The Star-Spangled Banner." That fairly routine request, however, produced an awkward moment several bars into the national anthem as two-thousand-plus Republicans searched the auditorium in vain for a flag toward which they could direct their adoration. Apparently, someone had neglected to bring the Star-Spangled Banner to the rally.

All is not well in East Texas.

The emcee quickly regrouped. "Look around you," he instructed the audience. "These are men and women of God who have come together on a Tuesday night in Longview, Texas, to say enough is enough!" Then he prayed for God's blessing on the assembly "as we move forward to take back East Texas for Jesus Christ."

The Religious Right is now in the midst of a generational transition of leadership. Some of the movement's founders have died or retired, and others, while still on the scene, have seen their influence wane. Robertson's intemperate comments have marginalized him somewhat within the movement, and his Christian Coalition has been rudderless since the departure in 1997 of Ralph Reed, who left to form his own political consulting firm and to plot his rise through the ranks of Georgia politics on his way to the White House. Ever since his failed attempt to take over the Praise the Lord (PTL) network in 1987, Jerry Falwell's empire has faced persistent financial crises, some of which have been eased with the help of Charles Keating Jr., whose savings-and-loan scandal during the Reagan years landed him in jail, and from Sun Myung Moon, head of the Unification Church. Falwell himself has descended to the level of self-parody; witness his comments following the September 11, 2001, terrorist attacks, which he blamed on "abortionists," feminists, and homosexuals, or his impassioned denunciation in 1999 of the *Teletubbies* character Tinky-Winky, which he described as a front for the gay-rights movement.

Although Robertson, Falwell, and others such as James Dobson have been reluctant to surrender the reins of power, the evangelical subculture has produced a new generation of conservative political activists hankering to step in. Rick Scarborough is one. Introduced in Longview as one of the "heroes of the faith," Scarborough bounced onto the stage and offered a prayer: "Lord, we pray that you would remove the judges who seek to destroy us."

Scarborough claims that he became a political activist after sitting in on an AIDS prevention assembly at his daughter's high school in Pearland, Texas. The presentation, he says, was peppered with sexually explicit references. Fuming, he returned to his church study and began plotting a strategy for reversing what he believes is America's headlong plunge into secularism. In 1998, Scarborough founded Vision America. The idea was to mobilize pastors around the country to engage politically by speaking out on political issues, registering voters in the church pews, and "leading their people to the polls."

By 2002, Vision America had become so successful in recruiting and organizing what Scarborough calls "patriot pastors" that he resigned his own pastorate to devote his energies full-time to the organization. In recent years, he has garnered a great deal of media attention for his political activities. Scarborough has been profiled in the *Washington Times*, the *Washington Post*, and *Time* magazine.[3]

In the course of his speech in Longview, Scarborough made a number of statements that would jangle the ears of those not already familiar with the red-meat rhetoric of the Religious Right. "Some things you do whether it's legal or not," he thundered, and he assured his audience that Tom DeLay, then the majority leader of the House of Representatives, was "a Christian man," despite the fact that he was under investigation for criminal activities and several ethics violations. But Scarborough's most astonishing statement of the evening was a simple, three-word sentence delivered offhandedly early in his address: "I am Baptist."

Indeed, as I learned later, Scarborough boasts impeccable Baptist credentials. A graduate of Houston Baptist University and Southwestern Baptist Theological Seminary, he was an itinerant evangelist before assuming the senior pastor position at First Baptist Church in Pearland, Texas, south of Houston, in 1990. He holds a Doctor of Ministry degree in "church growth" from Louisiana Baptist Theological Seminary. By his actions and his political agenda, however, Scarborough utterly misconstrues what it means to be Baptist.[4]

Baptists trace their history to the Anabaptist movement arising out of the Protestant Reformation in the sixteenth century. A number of Protestant leaders took seriously Martin Luther's admonition that the Bible alone was the believer's authority. Reading through the scriptures, these Protestants found no mention of children being baptized, so they insisted instead on adult (or believer's) baptism. This small band became known as Anabaptists—meaning to baptize again because they had already been baptized as infants

before their conversion to Baptist principles—and they were persecuted by both Catholic and Protestant authorities.

Anabaptists were, by necessity, a peripatetic people, fleeing their
oppressors through Europe and Russia and, finally, to North
America. (Some of the groups that trace their history to the Radical
Reformation include the Mennonites, the Amish, the Hutterites,
and the Brethren in Christ, among others.) The Baptist tradition in
England dates at least to the days of John Wycliffe in the fifteenth
century. As with the Anabaptist movement on the Continent, Baptists in England were persecuted as Dissenters from the Church of
England. For that reason, together with their fidelity to Jesus'
teachings about turning the other cheek, Baptists have always been
suspicious of entanglements with the state—at least until recently.

The Baptist tradition, then, enshrined two ideas: adult (as opposed to infant) baptism and liberty of individual conscience, generally expressed in the shorthand phrase "separation of church and
state." William Estep, for instance, one of the premier historians of
the Baptist tradition, wrote that, "It is impossible to define Baptists
apart from their devotion to the principle of complete religious
freedom." Roger Williams, founder of the Baptist tradition in
America, was a dissident in Puritan Massachusetts who was ex-
pelled from the colony in 1636 and went to Rhode Island to form a
religiously tolerant society.

It is to Williams that we owe the notion of religious disestablishment, the absence of a state church. Williams had witnessed the
miserable effects of religious establishment in Massachusetts,
where church leaders used the power of the government to enforce
their notions of orthodoxy. The entanglement of church and state,

Williams recognized, compromised the functions of both, although he was primarily concerned with protecting the purity of the church from the intrusions of the state into religious affairs. In his words, Williams wanted to shield the "garden" of the church from the "wilderness" of the world, and as a religious minority himself, he sought also to protect the rights of religious minorities from the government.

Williams expressed concern that any state endorsement of religion would diminish the authenticity of faith. Williams, addressing the Westminster Assembly in London in 1644, wondered aloud to his audience if the idolatry decried by the Hebrew prophets wasn't a dangerous conflation "of the several national and state religions that all nations set up."[5]

In 1663, Charles II granted the Charter of Rhode Island and Providence Plantations. This document enshrined Williams's Baptist principles of liberty of conscience. The people of Rhode Island aspired "to hold forth a lively experiment that a flourishing civil state may best be maintained among his Majesty's subjects with full religious liberty," the charter read, adding that "no person within the said colony shall hereafter be in any wise molested or called in question for any difference in opinion in matters of religion."[6]

Almost a century after Williams's death in 1684, Isaac Backus, another hero in the Baptist tradition, consolidated Williams's ideas on the separation of church and state, bringing them to the center of discussion during the formative years of the American republic. In an effort to overturn a Massachusetts law requiring all citizens of the state to pay an "ecclesiastical tax" to support the Congregational Church, Backus, a Baptist who had separated from the established Congregational Church in eighteenth-century New England, traveled to the Continental Congress in 1774 to make his case for religious disestablishment. He repeated his plea to the Massachusetts legislature, drawing a parallel to the Patriots' rhetoric of taxation without representation. He and his followers refused to pay the tax, he said, "not only upon your principles of not being taxed where we are not represented, but also because we dare not render that homage to any earthly power, which I and many of my brethren are fully convinced belongs only to God."[7]

Backus echoed Williams's dim view of government interventions in religion, and vice versa. Backus noted that Jesus himself "made no use of secular force in the first setting up of the Gospel-Church," even though he arguably could have used such help. "All acts of executive power in the civil state are to be performed in the name of the king or state they belong to," Backus wrote in his *Appeal to the Public for Religious Liberty* in 1773, "while all our religious acts are to be done in the *name of the Lord Jesus Christ* and so are to be performed *heartily as to the Lord and not unto men*." Can government enforce fidelity to the faith? Backus thought not: "it is but *lip service* and *vain worship* if our *fear toward [God] is taught by the precepts of men*."[8]

As colonists from several different nations and faiths arrived on America's shores, the Baptist model of religious disestablishment and liberty of conscience looked increasingly attractive in the eighteenth century. Representatives from groups other than the Baptists—Quakers, Presbyterians, Lutherans, Dutch Reformed, and others—took up the Baptist arguments for religious liberty. The presence of religious diversity, especially in the Middle Colonies of New York, New Jersey, and Pennsylvania, had forced colonial legislatures to make accommodations to the multiplicity of faiths. The Baptist model of church-state separation, then, offered an alternative to the religious establishments of Europe as the architects of the new nation contemplated how to configure church and state.

"It is not doubted but every man who wishes to be free will by all lawful ways in his power oppose the establishment of any one denomination in America," several Philadelphians wrote in 1768. "Religious establishments are very hardly kept from great corruption." When the Virginia House of Delegates sought to provide "for the legal support of Teachers of the Christian Religion," James Madison wrote his famous 1785 "Memorial and Remonstrance" to argue against any state endorsement of Christianity. "Who does not see that the same authority which can establish Christianity, in exclusion of all other religions, may establish with the same ease any particular sect of Christians, in exclusion of all other sects?" Madison asked. Like Williams before him, Madison worried that "the majority may trespass on the rights of the minority."[9]

Thomas Jefferson concurred with Madison that the government had no business dictating religious beliefs or practices. He counted Virginia's 1786 "Act for Establishing Religious Freedom" among his greatest achievements. "The opinions of men are not the object of civil government, nor under its jurisdiction," Jefferson wrote, "and to restrain the profession or propagation of principles on supposition of their ill tendency is a dangerous falacy [sic], which at once destroys all religious liberty." Jefferson was confident that "truth is great and will prevail if left to herself."[10]

It's not that the founders were antireligious. When Madison sent a draft of the Constitution to Jefferson, who was serving as the

American minister to France, Jefferson pronounced himself satisfied with the efforts of Madison and others. He went on, however,
to criticize "the omission of a bill of rights providing clearly and
without the aid of sophisms for the freedom of religion" and other
liberties. Although the beliefs of Jefferson and a few others tended
toward Deism, many of the founders held religious convictions
that we would recognize today as Christian orthodoxy. But as veterans of endless squabbles over religion in the Old World, some of
which had carried over to the colonies, the founders thought the
best posture would be for the government to stay out of the religion
business in the fledgling nation.[11]

Thus was born the grand and noble experiment of the First
Amendment, which both proscribes the establishment of religion and ensures the free exercise of religion. In devising it, the
founders called upon the ideas of Roger Williams as well as the
model of several of the Middle Colonies, including New York,
New Jersey, and Pennsylvania, all of which had demonstrated
that the way to accommodate religious pluralism was to avoid
religious establishment. "The notion of a Christian common-
wealth should be exploded forever," John Leland, yet another
Baptist, declared in 1790. "Government should protect every
man in thinking and speaking freely, and see that one does not
abuse another."[12]

The success of Rhode Island's experiment in church-state separation and religious liberty figured explicitly into the congres-
sional debates surrounding the proposed Bill of Rights in 1789,
discussions that produced the First Amendment: "Congress shall
make no law respecting an establishment of religion, or prohibiting the free exercise thereof." The line from Williams to the U.S.

Constitution, then, is unbroken. So durable and so successful was this formulation in delineating the boundaries between church and state that it remained intact throughout American history— until the rise of the Religious Right in the late 1970s.[13]

Despite Rick Scarborough's claims to be a Baptist, his message couldn't be more different from that of Roger Williams, founder of the tradition Scarborough claims as his own. Indeed, Scarborough is merely one of a whole phalanx of Religious Right leaders determined to eviscerate the First Amendment. Led by David Barton, head of an organization misleadingly called WallBuilders (a reference to the Hebrew prophet Nehemiah and the construction of the walls of Jerusalem, not the "wall of separation" between church and state), these Religious Right activists assert that religious disestablishment in America was never intended by the founders. Their tactics are remarkable for their lack of subtlety. Much like deniers of the Holocaust—though I am not suggesting any moral equivalency between the two—they simply deny that the First Amendment calls for the government to remain neutral on matters of faith, in spite of overwhelming historical and documentary evidence to the contrary.

Scarborough has picked up on this theme. "The whole concept of separation of church and state is a myth propagated by liberal judges," Scarborough told the *Houston Chronicle* in 2005. "It's not in the Constitution." Scarborough labels as "moral travesties" such issues as court rulings in defense of reproductive choice and same-sex marriage and against prayer in school and the posting of the Decalogue on public property. Scarborough even wrote a booklet (on sale at the back of the convention center) entitled *In Defense of Mixing Church and State*. The text is more screed than it is argument; it reads like something slapped together hurriedly. But since Scarborough styles himself an expert on the matter, and because of his growing stature as a leader of the Religious Right, this thirty-two-page pamphlet merits scrutiny.[14]

Scarborough opens with some fairly standard Religious Right complaints about the moral decline in American society. He then makes a statement with which I have no quarrel whatsoever, namely, that "Christians have an absolute mandate to take their Christianity into the market place of ideas and be salt and light." I suspect that Scarborough stumbled upon the metaphor of the *marketplace* quite by accident, but it is illuminating nonetheless. The metaphor of the marketplace is essential to understanding the role of the First Amendment in American life. By refusing to favor any religion or denomination as the state or established faith, the founders, in effect, set up a free market for religion in the United States. Without the assistance—or the impediment—of religious establishment, religious groups were free to compete with one another for popular followings. They no longer needed to worry that any one tradition enjoyed the favor of the state or that others would be subject to government sanctions.[15]

This notion was utterly unprecedented in Western culture, and not every religious leader thought that disestablishment was a good idea. Lyman Beecher, a Congregationalist minister in Litchfield, Connecticut, fought tirelessly against a plan to disestablish Congregationalism in Connecticut, fearing that religion would lose its influence in society. In 1820, however, within two years of disestablishment, Beecher was forced to repent. Disestablishment led not to the decline of the faith, but to a resurgence of religious sentiment. "Revivals now began to pervade the state," he wrote in his autobiography. "It cut the churches loose from dependence on state support. It threw them wholly on their own resources and on God." Beecher pronounced the separation of church and state "the best thing that ever happened to the State of Connecticut."[16]

As Beecher himself came to see, this radical idea of disestablishment has had an electrifying effect. Various religious groups—or entrepreneurs, to extend the free-market metaphor—have competed with one another throughout American history, thereby lending unparalleled energy and dynamism to America's religious marketplace. The percentage of Americans who believe in God or a supreme being—polls consistently place that number in the low to mid-nineties—far outstrips those of other nations. In Great Britain, the established Church of England draws less than 3 percent of the population to its doors. Leaders of the state Lutheran Church in Sweden petitioned parliament to be disestablished so that the church could enjoy the benefits of competing in the free marketplace of religion; disestablishment went into effect in January 2000. "I think we all see a stronger sense of commitment now," David Olson, pastor of St. Jacob's Church in Stockholm, said. "People realize it's up to them to maintain our churches, not the government." Observing the salutary effects of disestablishment in Sweden, ecclesiastical leaders in Norway now want to follow suit.

Given the resounding success of Williams's experiment in church-state separation, one would think that Baptists would be proud of their tradition's contribution to American society and to the vitality of religious life. Not Scarborough and his colleagues on the Religious Right. They would like nothing better than to dismantle the First Amendment. They want to live in an America where public prayer is mandated in public schools, where school vouchers support religious rather than secular public education, and where religious texts, such as the Ten Commandments, are prominently displayed in government-funded spaces such as courts and schools.[17]

Scarborough, parroting Barton and other leaders of the Religious Right, goes even further. Not only does he ignore Williams, his religious predecessor, but he denies altogether that the First Amendment calls for religious disestablishment. "A whole generation of Americans has grown up believing that the Constitution demands the separation of church and state," he laments. "That is simply a lie introduced by Satan and fostered by the courts." Scarborough explains, correctly, that the explicit "wall of separation" language comes not from the First Amendment but from Thomas Jefferson. On January 1, 1802, Jefferson responded to a letter from members of the Danbury Baptist Association, who expressed concerns about a rumor that a particular religious group would be designated as the national church. Jefferson, seeking to allay their fears, penned his classic and oft-quoted response. "I contemplate with solemn reverence," the president wrote, "that act of the whole American people which declared that their legislature should 'make no law respecting the establishment of religion, prohibiting the free exercise thereof,' thus building a wall of separation between church and State."[18]

Jefferson's letter to the Danbury Baptists in Connecticut has caused the Religious Right all manner of consternation in their attempts to subvert the disestablishment clause of the First Amendment. The first and most common rejoinder, one that Scarborough employs, is to point out that the phrase "separation of church and state" is not language found explicitly in the Constitution. True enough; it does come from Jefferson, who was paraphrasing Roger Williams. America's first Baptist warned God's people that when they open "a gap in the hedge or wall of Separation between the Garden of the Church and the Wilderness of the World, God hath ever broken down the wall itself . . . and made his Garden a Wilderness, as at this day."[19]

When Scarborough's argument breaks down, he relies on bluster. He asserts, without elaboration, that those who support the separation of church and state "have resorted to extracting nine words from a private correspondence to validate their views, which is foreign to the Constitution's original intent." They take Jefferson's words "out of context," Scarborough claims in his pamphlet, though he doesn't demonstrate in what way this is so. Never mind. Scarborough launches directly into his rant: "These facts are a moral outrage to our nation, and the resulting moral morass, apart from God's intervention, are [sic] irreversible."[20]

If Scarborough paid any attention to Roger Williams, his Baptist forebear, he would discover that Williams had issued some very harsh warnings about the dangers of church-state collusion. Williams insisted that political figures should not be empowered to adjudicate between competing religious faiths. He worried that, in a world in which church and state were entangled, "the civil magistrate must reform the church, establish religion, and so consequently must first judge and judicially determine which is true [and] which is false." Williams warned, finally, that state sponsorship of religion would yield an unhappy situation wherein "the whole world must rule and govern the Church."[21]

What if the state were able to establish the truest of true religions? Even if this were possible, Williams doubted that such a designation would have the desired effect. In fact, the consequence was likely to be the reverse. It is, Williams observed, "opposite to the souls of all men who by persecutions are ravished into a dissembled worship which their hearts embrace not." State-favored religion, moreover, was pointless, especially in the context of religious pluralism wrought by the Protestant Reformation. Reflecting on the futility of the government dictating belief, Williams asked, "Where find you evidence of a whole nation, country or kingdom converted to the faith, and of Christ's appointing of a whole nation or kingdom to walk in one way of religion?"[22]

"Soul liberty" lay at the foundation of Williams's political philosophy, and it remains—ostensibly at least—one of the cornerstones of Baptist beliefs. Soul liberty protected individual conscience from the tyranny of the majority, a principle that Baptists, at least until recently, have always defended, in part because Baptists themselves began as a minority. Now that Baptists have achieved numerical success in America—the Southern Baptist Convention is the largest Protestant denomination, and it approaches hegemonic status in the South—so-called Baptists like Scarborough want to rescind the principle of soul liberty.

Those who seek to abrogate the First Amendment separation of church and state, however, fail to comprehend both the teachings of Jesus and the lessons of history. As Backus noted, Jesus did not have the benefit of the state when he formed his church, yet Christianity flourished nevertheless, ultimately reaching beyond Palestine to the farthest corners of the earth. The umbrella of state sanction beginning with the conversion of Constantine in A.D. 312 turned out to be, at best, a mixed blessing, opening the door to state interference in religious matters. An era known as the Dark Ages ensued, and by the sixteenth century, the church had become so corrupted by power that it would eventually take Martin Luther and the unleashing of the Protestant Reformation to renew it.

Having ignored both Roger Williams and Isaac Backus, his Baptist predecessors, Scarborough snubbed yet another Baptist icon: George Washington Truett. One of the most influential leaders of the Southern Baptist Convention, Truett graduated from Baylor University in 1897 and promptly became pastor of the First Baptist Church in Dallas, Texas. Over the course of his tenure there, the congregation grew from 715 to 7,804. Truett was both an eloquent preacher and a forceful proponent of Baptist teachings; he served as president of the Southern Baptist Convention from 1927 to 1929.

On May 16, 1920, Truett ascended the east steps of the Capitol Building in Washington, D.C., to issue a forceful apology for the Baptist principle of church-state separation. On that Sunday afternoon, an audience of ten to fifteen thousand awaited his words. Truett opened with a paean to the United States, and he declared that "the supreme contribution of the new world to the old is the contribution of religious liberty." Indeed, it was "the chiefest contribution that America has thus far made to civilization," and Truett was proud to announce that the separation of church and state was "preeminently a Baptist achievement."

Truett continued with a ringing endorsement of Baptist principles, especially civil and religious liberty. Baptists affirmed, he said, "the natural and fundamental and indefeasible right of every human being to worship God or not, according to the dictates of his conscience, and, as long as he does not infringe upon the rights of others, he is to be held accountable alone to God for all religious beliefs and practices." This principle extends beyond mere toleration of others and their beliefs to absolute liberty of conscience: "Toleration is a concession, while liberty is a right."

Like Backus before him, Truett interpreted the era after Constantine as disastrous for the church. "When Christianity first found its way into the city of the Ceasars it lived at first in cellars and alleys," he said, "but when Constantine crowned the union of church and state, the church was stamped with the spirit of the Caesars." Religion, Truett insisted, should be voluntary. "It is the consistent and insistent contention of our Baptist people, always and everywhere, that religion must be forever voluntary and uncoerced, and that it is not the prerogative of any power, whether civil or ecclesiastical, to compel men to conform to any religious creed or form of worship," he thundered. According to Truett, Baptists recognized that enjoying religious liberty for themselves entailed defending it for others. "A Baptist would rise at midnight to plead for absolute religious liberty," he declared, "for his Catholic neighbor, and for his Jewish neighbor, and for everybody else."

"God wants free worshipers and no other kind," he proclaimed. "Christ's religion needs no prop of any kind from any worldly source, and to the degree that it is thus supported is a millstone hanged about its neck."

The subject of millstones brings us back to the convention center in Longview, Texas, to the second featured speaker of the evening,

Roy S. Moore, formerly the chief justice of the Supreme Court of the state of Alabama, better known as the "Ten Commandments Judge."

Rick Scarborough introduced Moore as a "brilliant jurist" and remarked, "If God would give us a thousand men like that in the court house and the church house, we'd see a revival." Moore stepped to the podium and immediately began reciting a lengthy passage from Samuel Adams, one of the founders, in an address before the Continental Congress in 1776. "It is indeed an honor to be here, and I sincerely mean that," Moore intoned. "But I would gladly have declined an honor to which I find myself unequal. I have not the calmness and impartiality which the infinite importance of this occasion demands. I will not deny the charge of mine enemies that resentment for the accumulated injuries of our country, and an ardour for her glory, rising to enthusiasm, may deprive me of that accuracy of judgment and expression which men of cooler passions may possess. Let me beseech you, then, to hear me with caution, to examine without prejudice, and to correct the mistakes into which I may be hurried by my zeal."

After Scarborough's rousing introduction of the judicial celebrity standing before them, the audience clearly wanted to be impressed, but they sat in a kind of stunned and befuddled silence at the portentous solemnity of Moore's opening. The former judge quickly shifted to more familiar rhetoric that he knew would stir the crowd. America, Moore said, was "a nation founded on God," adding, "God gives us our rights; he created us."

Roy Stewart Moore, who, like Scarborough, claims to be a Baptist, graduated from the U.S. Military Academy at West Point in 1969. After military service as a military policeman in Vietnam, where he was known, not affectionately, as "Captain America" for his zeal, Moore returned to Alabama and earned his law degree in 1977 from the University of Alabama. After a stint as a deputy district attorney in Etowah County, he ran for office, a circuit court judgeship, but was defeated badly. In an effort to regroup, he headed then for Texas to embark on a career as a professional kickboxer and then to the outback of Australia.

Moore returned to Alabama in 1984 and briefly set up private practice in Gadsden. He was then appointed to fill a vacant circuit court judgeship in Gadsden; he ran and won election to the bench in his own right in 1992. Moore opened his court sessions with prayer and hung a hand-carved wooden plaque depicting the Ten Commandments in his courtroom. Moore's critics claimed that the plaque represented an infringement of the disestablishment clause of the First Amendment. The American Civil Liberties Union (ACLU) filed suit in 1995 to have the plaque removed. The people of Alabama, however, rather than censure his flouting of the Constitution, rewarded Moore by electing him chief justice of the Alabama Supreme Court in 2000. Moore, running as a Republican, had campaigned for office as the "Ten Commandments Judge."

Shortly after his election, Moore commissioned a local gravestone company to produce a monument, emblazoned with the Decalogue, using a block of granite from Barre, Vermont, considered the finest in the world. Late in the evening of July 31, 2001, Moore and a work crew, laboring through the night, installed the two-and-a-half-ton monument in the lobby of the Alabama Judicial Building in Montgomery. The monument came to be known as "Roy's Rock," or, simply, "The Rock."

Because he had run for office as the Ten Commandments Judge, Moore's action surprised no one. The ACLU had warned against it as an unconstitutional infringement of the disestablishment clause of the First Amendment. Other groups, religious and otherwise (including the Alabama Free Thought Association), had petitioned to have representations of *their* convictions posted in the Alabama Judicial Building. Due to the proximity of the building to the Dexter Avenue Baptist Church just up the street, others suggested mounting a plaque with Martin Luther King's "I Have a Dream" speech on the walls of the Judicial Building. Moore steadfastly refused all such entreaties. He wanted only the Decalogue.

As it had threatened, the ACLU brought action, joined in the case by Americans United for the Separation of Church and State and the Southern Poverty Law Center. Myron Thompson, U.S. district judge, heard arguments in October 2002. Moore testified that the "Judeo-Christian God" is the only true God of the one true religion and that he presides over both the state and the church. That God, he insisted, is above all other gods because he provides the freedom of conscience that allows people to worship other faiths.

Judge Thompson rendered his verdict on November 18, 2002: By installing the monument and refusing to allow equivalent expressions of alternative religious beliefs, Moore had violated the disestablishment clause of the First Amendment. By favoring one religious tradition above all others, Roy's Rock represented a religious statement and not, as Moore had claimed, merely an acknowledgement of the roots of American jurisprudence.

Thompson ordered the monument removed. Moore filed an appeal with the U.S. Court of Appeals and the Supreme Court, but both refused to hear the case. He then vowed to defy the law. Moore's colleagues on the bench approved the removal of the monument to a storage closet, which was finally accomplished in August 2003. The Court of the Judiciary then heard arguments about the still-defiant chief justice and decided unanimously on November 13, 2003, to remove Moore from office for flouting federal law and violating his oath to uphold the Constitution of the United States.[23]

The removal of Roy's Rock to a storage closet in the Alabama Judicial Building was a source of consternation to many of his followers, some of whom had frantically protested to the bitter end. Since Moore had installed the monument two years earlier, scores of buses had pulled up to the Judicial Building and disgorged the faithful. They would file into the lobby, drop to their knees, and pray in front of the granite monument. Its removal precipitated all manner of wailing and gnashing of teeth on the part of conservatives—some far beyond the Alabama borders—many of whom identified themselves as Baptists.

Many on the Religious Right viewed the removal of Roy's Rock as clear evidence of America's moral decline. In a hysterical missive circulated by e-mail, one protester predicted that the depiction of Moses and the Ten Commandments on the U.S. Supreme Court Building in Washington, D.C., would soon disappear. Another of Moore's supporters in Montgomery loudly declared that if you wanted to see the future of America—by which he meant, presumably, a future devoid of religious sentiment—consider the blank space in the lobby of the Judicial Building where Roy's Rock once sat.

One protester trumped all others. "Get your hands off my God!" he screamed upon learning that the court had ordered the monument's removal.

Since losing his position on the Alabama Supreme Court, Moore has traveled the country in an effort to burnish his credentials as a martyr. Friends and supporters established an organization, the Foundation of Moral Law, to provide a cushion and to supply the former chief justice with a bodyguard, an office and staff in a prominent Montgomery building, and expenses for travel. On October 3, 2005, Moore announced his candidacy for governor of Alabama, challenging the incumbent governor, Robert Riley, for the nomination of the Republican Party.

At the convention center in Longview, Moore recounted the Ten Commandments saga—the monument, its removal, and his removal from office for failure to obey the court order. He promised the audience, as he has to Religious Right rallies around the nation, "I would do it again."

Like Scarborough, Moore calls himself a Baptist, but Roy's Rock represents an utter repudiation of Baptist principles. Roger Williams, Isaac Backus, and George Washington Truett all affirmed that religion functions best without the endorsement of the state. They also recognized the rights of minorities and the importance of liberty of conscience. Williams had written that "true civility and Christianity may both flourish in a state or kingdom, notwithstanding the permission of divers and contrary consciences."[24]

Despite all the hysteria at the Judicial Building in Montgomery, the legal decision to remove the monument was the proper one, both to protect the state from sectarianism and to protect the faith from government sanction. "I do not believe it is for the interest of religion to invite the civil magistrate to direct its exercises, its discipline, or its doctrines," Jefferson wrote in 1808. The depiction of Moses and the Ten Commandments will not be chiseled from the U.S. Supreme Court Building anytime soon because, unlike Roy's Rock in Alabama, the frieze in Washington portrays one of several sources for American jurisprudence—and those sources are numerous, including the Code of Hammurabi, Confucius, and the English Common Law tradition.[25]

Moore, on the other hand, sought to enshrine only one source, and he steadfastly, even belligerently, refused to recognize any others. On that basis, Judge Thompson concluded that both the intent and the effect of the monument were to give the place of honor to one tradition, to the exclusion of all others. That, clearly, represents a violation of the First Amendment proscription against religious establishment.

Moore styles himself an "originalist" in his approach to the Constitution, a term that is part of the coded language used by the Religious Right and by conservatives generally. Much like those evangelicals who take a mechanistic approach to interpreting the scriptures, an "originalist" holds that the Constitution is not a fluid and pliable document, that it should be interpreted according to the "original intent" of the framers.

Originalism, first popularized by Edwin Meese, Ronald Reagan's attorney general, and by Robert Bork, Reagan's failed 1987 nominee to the Supreme Court, espouses the narrowest possible reading of the Constitution. It is often invoked to advance the neo-conservative agenda. Most specifically, conservatives have drawn on this doctrine in an effort to discredit the Supreme Court's *Roe v. Wade* decision of 1973, the ruling that guaranteed legal access to abortion on the grounds that individual privacy was a constitutional right. Opponents of abortion seized on this, using the originalist language to argue that the framers of the Constitution never intended to guarantee individual privacy, and, therefore, women have no such rights.[26]

Moore also invokes the original intent of the founders in his crusade against the First Amendment, but to rather different ends. He asserts that when the founders talked about "free exercise of religion" they meant Christianity—or, in his more expansive moments, Moore extends the guarantee to what he calls the "Judeo-Christian tradition." Because the framers had no experience of, say, Muslims or Hindus or Daoists, Moore argues, their "original intent" was to secure for Americans the free exercise of Christianity alone. Under this originalist interpretation, in Moore's view, the First Amendment guarantees the free exercise of *Christianity* or the "Judeo-Christian tradition." No other religious expression, according to Moore's originalist scheme, enjoys the protection of the U.S. Constitution. For this reason, Moore argues, his refusal to accommodate similar displays representing other faiths is completely in keeping with the ideas of the founders and the Constitution they created.

Originalism is compelling for its clarity and its simplicity; Antonin Scalia and Clarence Thomas frequently invoke it in their Supreme Court opinions. But the limits of originalism become apparent when you try to apply it to the second clause of the First Amendment, the guarantee of a free press. Employing the same logic that Moore uses to justify the exclusion of religious expressions other than Christianity—and, perhaps, Judaism—you would have to argue that freedom of the press extends strictly and exclusively to newspapers, because newspapers were the only "press" that the framers knew at the end of the eighteenth century. A documentary filmmaker, then, or a television journalist, according to this narrow, originalist view, could not claim a constitutional guarantee to freedom of the press because the framers did not have television in mind when they drafted the First Amendment.

The Religious Right's attempt to eviscerate the First Amendment is profoundly ironic inasmuch as evangelicals themselves, and Baptists in particular, have been the primary beneficiaries of disestablishment in America. They operated outside of the New England religious establishment in the seventeenth and eighteenth centuries, and the explosion of Baptist growth in the nineteenth century would have been impossible—or, at least considerably more difficult—without the protections of the First Amendment, its proscription against religious establishment, and its guarantee of free exercise. During the early decades of the nineteenth century, Baptists competed with other religious denominations in the South, especially the Presbyterians and the Methodists, and carved for themselves a presence that approaches hegemony.

Quite apart from all of the legal arguments concerning the First Amendment and the separation of church and state, and even beyond the overwhelming evidence that religious life has flourished in America as nowhere else precisely because of religious disestablishment, the even larger argument against conflating church and state is an argument that evangelicals know very well: the dangers of trivialization. Throughout American history, evangelicals have been extraordinarily suspicious of formalism and empty ritual. True religion, evangelicals have always believed, functions best outside of institutional constraints. When Theodorus Jacobus Frelinghuysen, a Dutch Pietist, arrived in New York City from the Netherlands in 1720, for instance, he castigated a fellow minister for using the Lord's Prayer in Dutch Reformed worship services, remarking that such empty ritual utterances were inimical to true piety. The holiness movement of the nineteenth century, to cite another of many examples, was a reaction against the perceived complacency of Methodism, which itself had arisen out of an earlier effort to revitalize the Church of England. All of these evangelicals deplored rote expressions of religious sentiment as disingenuous.

How peculiar, then, given this history, that evangelicals associated with the Religious Right would seek to enshrine Christianity as the faith of the nation through prescribed prayer in schools and government support for religious education or by erecting religious monuments on government property, thereby projecting the appearance, if not the reality, of state sanction. Evangelicals, especially Baptists, know better. They have always opposed formalized prayer as empty ritual, what one eighteenth-century evangelical called the "old, rotten, and stinking routine of religion." Jesus instructed his followers not to pray "like the hypocrites," who pray "on the street corners to be seen by others." Evangelicals throughout American history have preached against the dangers of trivializing the faith, and what could be more inimical to true piety than the recitation of prayers prescribed by the state or the fetishization of the "Judeo-Christian tradition" on a block of granite in a public building?[27]

Where have all the *real* Baptists gone? From Williams to Backus to Truett and throughout American history, at least until recently, Baptists have been fierce guardians of the First Amendment and the separation of church and state. Several related developments in the late 1970s combined to undermine that noble tradition: the rise of the Religious Right, paradoxically during the presidential administration of a Southern Baptist, Jimmy Carter; the conservative takeover of America's largest Protestant denomination, the Southern Baptist Convention, in 1979; and the rise in popularity of an ideology called Reconstructionism. The effects of the first were felt almost immediately. The Religious Right proved decisive in the presidential election of 1980 and was a major force four years later.

If the effects of the Religious Right were dramatic and easily discernible, the seizure of the Southern Baptists by conservatives, however, was more gradual, its effects evolutionary rather than revolutionary. In plotting their action in the late 1970s, the architects of the takeover of the Southern Baptist Convention recognized that the president of the convention had broad appointive powers over denominational agencies and even to the trustee boards of colleges and seminaries affiliated with the convention.

Beginning with the election of Adrian Rogers, pastor of Bellevue Baptist Church outside of Memphis, Tennessee, in 1979, conservatives have elected other conservatives to the presidency in an unbroken line up to the present. Each president has used his appointive powers to turn back what conservatives regard as the drift toward liberalism within the Southern Baptist Convention.

But the new conservative leadership didn't stop there. Lured by the prospect of political power during the Reagan years, the leaders of the Southern Baptist Convention steadily whittled away at their Baptist heritage and moved the denomination into the orbit of the Religious Right. Instead of advocating the separation of church and state, they supported prescribed, compulsory prayer in public schools and, more recently, federal funding for faith-based initiatives and school vouchers for private education, including religious schools. Whereas Truett, a past president of the Southern Baptist Convention, had used his prominence to defend Baptist principles of church-state separation, his successors since 1979 have sought instead to undermine those principles.

In order to justify their radical tack to the right, Baptists drew on an ideology called Reconstructionism as a way of rationalizing the abandonment of Baptist principles. Reconstructionism, also called "theonomy" or "dominion theology," is a social ethic popular among leaders of the Religious Right that advocates restructuring civil society according to the laws contained in the Hebrew Bible. Devised in the early 1960s by Rousas John Rushdoony, Reconstructionism seeks to rewrite civil and criminal codes to conform to Mosaic and Levitical laws in the Old Testament.

Reconstructionists believe that capital punishment, for instance, should be imposed for everything from sodomy to incorrigibility in children. Rushdoony, who was active in the archconservative John Birch Society, published the "bible" of Reconstructionism in 1973, a nine-hundred-page volume entitled *The Institutes of Biblical Law*, and his writings are laced with racism and anti-Semitism. Reconstructionists especially detest the notion of toleration. Gary

North, who was Rushdoony's estranged son-in-law and who remains one of the movement's most militant spokesmen, has insisted that "the perfect love of God necessarily involves the perfect hatred of God's enemies." Rushdoony himself openly resented the fact that "in the name of toleration, the believer is asked to associate on a common level of total acceptance with the atheist, the pervert, the criminal, and the adherents of other religions."

Religious Right leaders such as Scarborough; Pat Robertson; Jerry Falwell, founder of Moral Majority; Richard Land, head of the Southern Baptist Ethics and Religious Liberty Commission; and Randall Terry, the radical antiabortionist and founder of Operation Rescue—all of whom claim to be Baptists—have been especially infatuated with Rushdoony's ideas. They have seized on such statements as "regenerate man works to re-establish the law order of God among men, to establish church, state, and society in terms of the word of God, and to manifest the kingdom of God in every meaning."[28]

Reconstructionists, in short, don't want to reconfigure the line of separation between church and state. They want to obliterate it altogether. "Democracy is the great love of the failures and cowards of life," Rushdoony wrote. "The state has a duty to serve God, to be Christian, to be a part of God's kingdom, or else it shall be judged by Him."[29]

Although Rushdoony died in 2001, his Reconstructionist agenda is still propagated by the Chalcedon Foundation, which he founded in 1964. Reconstructionism also lives on in the ideology of so-called Baptists like Robertson, Falwell, Land, Scarborough, and Moore. In October 2003, for instance, at the height of Moore's legal troubles, the Chalcedon Foundation published a defense of the Alabama chief justice and Roy's Rock; it was written by an associate professor of law at Falwell's Liberty University.

The Baptist tradition couldn't be more opposed to these Reconstructionist ideas. Roger Williams and Isaac Backus represented religious minorities who looked to the government for protection from the entrenched, established majority. Their putative descendants, however, seek to impose their religious views on all Americans, thereby violating not only the First Amendment but the very principles that define their own religious heritage.

What Scarborough and Moore and their supporters fail to recognize, apparently, is the lesson that Lyman Beecher learned only belatedly: that religious disestablishment as mandated by the First Amendment is the best friend religion ever had. Religion has thrived in this country for more than two centuries precisely because the state has (for the most part, at least) stayed out of the religion business. Religious establishment breeds complacency. The examples of other Western nations suggest that once you begin to dictate religious belief or behavior, as with prescribed prayer in schools or Roy's Rock in Montgomery, Alabama, you kill it.

How outrageous that Rick Scarborough, Roy Moore, and many of their followers claim to be Baptists! I want to know why every Baptist in the state of Alabama didn't storm the Judicial Building after Moore installed his monument and demand that it be removed immediately, not merely because the monument itself became the subject of a kind of perverse idolatry—I wonder if Moore's followers remember the Golden Calf—but, more basically, because it violated bedrock Baptist principles of soul liberty and freedom of individual conscience. Shame on every Baptist in Alabama who sat by silently and put up with this nonsense!

Quite properly, Roy's Rock was removed from the lobby of Alabama's Judicial Building. The First Amendment prevailed over religious sectarianism and political chicanery. Still, I do think it's a shame that this imposing block of granite, the size and girth of a washing machine, was consigned to a storage room. The appropriate place for such a monument might be in one of Montgomery's many churches or even in Moore's front yard, as an expression of his personal convictions. Let him deal with the neighbors and the zoning board rather than tampering with the Constitution and the venerable tradition of church-state separation.

Those of us who number ourselves in the community of faith must resist the blandishments of the culture. The lesson of the Protestant Reformation, and perhaps of the New Testament itself, is the treachery of institutions as guarantors of faith. Indeed, one of the reasons for evangelical success throughout American history is the alacrity with which evangelicals have found creative ways to operate outside of institutional boundaries, be it the open-air preaching of George Whitefield in the eighteenth century, the circuit riders of the nineteenth, or the innovative use of media by Aimee Semple McPherson, Charles Fuller, and Billy Graham in the twentieth. Conversely, perhaps the greatest weakness of mainline Protestantism in recent decades is its misplaced faith in and allegiance to institutions. This reliance on denominational structures and apparatus has enervated religious vitality and commitment, in part because it breeds complacency, the very danger inherent in religious establishment.

Like Jesus standing on the ramparts overlooking the city, evangelicals must somehow find the courage and the will to resist the devil's cajoling, the temptations of authority and splendor and power and arrogance and cultural influence. We must recognize that religion flourishes best at the margins of society and not at the centers of power. A granite monument in Alabama trivializes the faith and makes the Decalogue into a fetish. Let's recall the words of one protester on the steps of the Alabama Judicial Building: "Get your hands off my God!" If I'm not mistaken, one of the commandments chiseled into that granite block warns against graven images. Addressing the Westminster Assembly about the dangers of state endorsement of religion, Roger Williams remarked in 1644 about "how impossible it is for a dead stone to have fellowship with the living God."[30]

I came to Texas in search of Baptists. What irony! There at the heart of Baptist country, Baptist principles regarding the separation of church and state have all but disappeared. What was once a proud and mighty—and defining—tradition of ensuring that government did not interfere with religion and religion did not meddle with government has withered beneath the onslaughts of misguided individuals who seek to impose their own views on the rest of society. The gospel is compromised, American Protestantism is imperiled, and the republic itself suffers from the massive disappearance of Baptists from the American landscape.

Never in my life did I think I would say this, but America needs more Baptists—*real* Baptists, not counterfeit Baptists like Roy Moore or Rick Scarborough or Richard Land or Jerry Falwell, all of whom are Baptists in name only. Our nation loses something very crucial as Baptists vanish from the American landscape. "The

Baptists were the first propounders of absolute liberty," John Locke once observed, "just and true liberty, equal and impartial liberty."

Christianity itself needs more Baptists, women and men willing to reconnect with the scandal of the gospel and not chase after the chimera of state sanction. We need women and men prepared to stand on conviction and articulate the faith in the midst of a pluralistic culture, not by imposing their principles on the remainder of society but by following the example of Jesus and doing what Baptists have always done best: preaching the gospel and not lusting after temporal power and influence.

Roy's Rock was consigned to a darkened storeroom, out of the public eye. It was shoved aside, along with other graven images throughout history. The gospel, however, endures. And it survives not because it has been idolized in a block of granite or because politicians deign to give it their blessing. It survives for the same reason it flourished in first-century Palestine and throughout the centuries—because believers have borne witness to its transformative power. Some of the best of these—we call them Baptists—have stoutly resisted the temptation to impose their understanding of the faith on others through the coercive mechanisms of the state.

"Baptists have one consistent record concerning liberty throughout their long and eventful history," George Washington Truett declared from the steps of the Capitol in 1920. "They have never been a party to oppression of conscience."

May it again be so. May it always be so.

chapter 3

Deconstructing Democracy

School Vouchers, Homeschooling, and
the War on Public Education

*This is our choice: to abandon public schools, or
to redeem them. My choice is clear: I argue for
redemption. I argue that America's central cities
have had enough of abandonment. They have been
abandoned by big business, abandoned by the middle
class, abandoned by high-paying jobs, abandoned by
major supermarket chains, and on and on. Only two
institutions remain to anchor inner-city communities:
the churches and the public schools. It would be ironic
and tragic if we now chose to abandon one of those two
anchors, the public schools.*
—REG WEAVER, VICE PRESIDENT OF THE
NATIONAL EDUCATION ASSOCIATION, 1999

GRANT FRANKE'S SOCIAL STUDIES CLASS opens with prayer.
Eight wiggly middle schoolers suddenly ceased their chatter and
fell silent. "I pray for my family and for my best friend's mom," a
student in the front row intoned. "I pray for my friends. In Jesus'
name. Amen."

Franke's lesson plan for this Monday morning called for a discussion of cattle drives in the Old West. He approached the topic with Socratic-style questions and answers, good cheer, and the youthful verve of a recent college graduate, which he is. His persona morphs into Señor Franke for Spanish-language instruction later in the day, but during social studies, he expended his energies trying to make middle schoolers understand the dynamics of herding cattle to market in the nineteenth century. Toward the end of class, Franke, in what appeared to be a sudden burst of inspiration, invited all eight students to huddle with him in the corner of the classroom to simulate the crowded conditions in the holding pen.

Portraits of every U.S. president filled the panel above the blackboard in Franke's classroom, and a handwritten poster behind the teacher spelled out the "Class Rules":

1. Follow Jesus
2. Respect
3. Raise hand, wait to be called on, talk one at a time
4. Keep track of supplies & stuff
5. Stay in your seat
6. Only handshakes, hi-fives & daps
7. Be honest
8. Do your homework

Signs and posters adorned every wall of the classroom. A small one read, "God is in control," and a larger sign listed the Ten Commandments. On another wall, an extensive chart in the form of a poster titled "Creation & Evolution" contained the following column headings: "What the Theory of Evolution Says," "What

Evolutionists Say We Ought to See," "What We Actually Observe in Nature," "What Scientists Say," and "Explanations Offered by Creationists."

Down the corridor in the science classroom, a teacher distributed copies of the *Cleveland Plain Dealer* to the seven students and asked them to read a front-page story entitled "Green Space Losing Ground." Amid the predictable middle-school murmurs, the teacher suggested, "You can't read and talk at the same time." A voice shot back reflexively, "Yes, I can!" One of the posters on the wall read, "Our God is an awesome God," and another quoted Genesis 1:1 against a beautiful *National Geographic*-like photograph: "In the beginning God created the heavens and the earth." At the front of the classroom, an empty cross hung in the center of the wall, flanked by an American flag in the left-hand corner and a red, white, and blue Christian flag in the right.

The library and learning center at West Park Lutheran School in Cleveland, Ohio, has about it the air of congenial dishevelment. Seven desktop computers of fairly recent vintage line the row of windows. A sign above one of them reads, "We will honor God in all things." Titles on the shelves range from *Treasure Island* and *Marjorie Stoneman Douglas: Friend of the Everglades* to *Jesus and His Times* and *Luther's Small Catechism*.

The principal of the school, Nancy Clark, is a diminutive woman with salt-and-pepper hair and a kind smile. After several phone calls to arrange my visit, I finally met her earlier that morning as she was preparing to step in as a substitute for the seventh-grade religion class (the pastor had left a message and begged off). Although Clark had confided to me that she hadn't the slightest idea what she would teach, she whisked confidently into the learning center half an hour later. She had the students read aloud a passage from Matthew 18 and then divided them into three groups of four to plan skits illustrating the principles for conflict resolution derived from the biblical lesson. The students at West Park clearly enjoy an easy camaraderie with one another. Even when one boy landed an all-too-realistic punch on another student in the playacting, the entire class, including the victim, erupted in laughter. "Let's close with prayer," Clark said at the end of the period. A girl named Jessie volunteered. "Dear Lord, thank you for this day," she began, before rehearsing the lesson of the morning, Jesus' command to forgive one another.

West Park Lutheran School draws its support from four Lutheran churches in Cleveland, all of them part of the theologically and socially conservative Lutheran Church—Missouri Synod denomination, a group with a long history of commitment to religious education. The four congregations run both an elementary school and a middle school, West Park, which uses the facilities of Mount Calvary Evangelical Lutheran Church, located on Lorain Avenue, one of the main arteries of the city. The building that houses West Park School was constructed in 1926, and the adjacent church sanctuary, made of dun-colored bricks, went up in 1959.

As with many inner-city areas, the neighborhood has changed in recent years, due to the shifting tectonics of race, religion, and economics. A boarded-up firehouse sits adjacent to the school's parking lot, mute testimony to shrinking municipal budgets, and tall chain-link fences cordon the neighborhood into small parcels. Across Lorain Avenue from the school, the bilingual sign above a storefront advertises "Holyland Imports" in both English and Arabic; one large sign in the window reads "Halal Meat" and another, "Whole Goats." Omar's Hair Design and Assad's Bakery are nearby. Sahara Restaurant, which features Lebanese food, sits a block away.

West Park is facing tough times in this pluralistic environment. The school enrolled 80 students in the 2005–2006 school year, down from 129 the year before. A large sign facing the street in front of the school advertises for students:

NOW ENROLLING
Grades K–8
Vouchers Accepted

"We'd have to close if we didn't have the vouchers," Clark confided. The church once provided the school with a subsidy of $2,000 a month, Clark said, but that has since dropped to $750. Even so, the congregation, which now has only seventy active members, is three months behind on its payments.

In the mid-1990s, the state of Ohio began allowing parents to use school vouchers to pay for their children's education in private and religious schools. The measure has been a blessing for West Park, where tuition runs $2,800 a year. The taxpayers of Ohio provide any student who wants it an education voucher worth $2,250 a year. Of the students at West Park Lutheran School, 80 percent use the vouchers.

Across town, the windowless doors on the Walton School greet visitors with two large signs, one in Spanish and the other in English:

NOTICE
It is illegal to carry a firearm, deadly weapon,
or dangerous ordnance anywhere on these premises.

On each sign a diagonal line crosses an image of a handgun inside a red circle.

Dolly Goodwin's sixth-grade classroom is considerably more congested than the middle-school rooms at West Park Lutheran School. Twenty-seven students, fresh from lunch, milled about in a kind of energetic, amiable chaos. Goodwin called them to order several times, raising her voice against the din. She directed their attention to two volunteers from the AmeriCorps "City Year" program, who presented a self-esteem and abstinence program, focusing this day on the use and abuse of marijuana.[1]

During the presentation, Goodwin, who holds a doctorate from Ohio State University, prepared for another of her classes at the back of the room. An imposing woman with a no-nonsense demeanor in her dealings with the students, Goodwin looks younger than her sixty years. She has taught in the Cleveland system for her entire career, except for a stint of several years as head of a Catholic school. During a whispered exchange at the back of the classroom, Goodwin conceded that she was "putting my time in" so that she can retire from the Cleveland schools. But, inveterate teacher that she is, she expects that she will nonetheless eventually teach somewhere else.

Out of the twenty-seven students in Goodwin's classroom, only one was Anglo, and another, African American; everyone else was Hispanic. When I remarked on the contrast between the eight-student, overwhelmingly white classroom at West Park Lutheran

School and the twenty-seven students in her charge, Goodwin noted that public money for education was going increasingly to religious schools and to charter schools. The voucher system, she said, was bleeding the Cleveland Municipal School District, but "the charter schools are the real problem" because they divert education funds and siphon off the best students to privately run institutions. The charter schools and the voucher schools can choose which students they want to educate, whereas public schools must accept all students, including those from less-affluent households and those with physical, mental, or emotional disabilities.

Goodwin sought to dispel the notion that students learned about values only in religious schools. "I have to teach them what is morally right, no matter what the system," she said. Goodwin believes that it is incumbent upon her to reinforce each student's faith, regardless of his particular religious tradition. "I tell the parents at the beginning of every year," she said, "that I will teach your child what is morally right until I'm dead."

In 1995, the Ohio general assembly approved the pilot voucher plan for Cleveland, a measure that provided state funds for students to opt out of public education and attend a private school. A year earlier, David L. Brennan, an Akron businessman well connected in Republican circles and a major contributor to Republican candidates, had proposed a voucher system for the state. It happened that Brennan had already established a corporation, Hope for Cleveland's Children, which was even then evaluating five sites in Cleveland for the construction of for-profit charter schools. The rationale for vouchers, presented by Brennan and other opponents of public education who styled themselves advocates of "school choice," was that students ill-served in public schools could use the vouchers to transfer into private schools and thereby obtain a better education.

Brennan pressed his argument on the Republican-dominated general assembly. The measure prevailed and was signed into law by George V. Voinovich, also a Republican, on June 30, 1995. Although Milwaukee, Wisconsin, had instituted a voucher program in 1990, the Ohio program differed in that it allowed public money to go to religious schools. Indeed, more than 96 percent of the funds from the publicly financed voucher program ended up in the coffers of religious institutions. Two years following the passage of the voucher legislation, Brennan was back, eager to expand the voucher program into public support for private schools. He persuaded the general assembly and Voinovich to expand the "school choice" program to include charter schools.

Because Ohio's voucher and charter school program directed taxpayer money to religious schools, the program faced a series of court challenges. One suit was brought by the American Federation of Teachers and a coalition of parent groups, school administrators, and civil libertarians; a second challenge was filed by People for the American Way, the Ohio branch of the American Civil Liberties Union, and Americans United for the Separation of Church and State. "The best cure for Cleveland's school problems would be to create higher academic standards and higher standards of conduct for all of Cleveland's public school students," the head of the American Federation of Teachers said. "These are the things parents want for their children in school, and these are the things teachers know work. That's where improvement efforts should focus, not on a radical experiment with no evidence to support it."[2]

In the Franklin County Court of Common Pleas, Judge Lisa Sadler ruled in July 1996 in favor of the programs. They did not violate the First Amendment's proscription against religious establishment, she wrote, because "nonpublic sectarian schools participating in the scholarship program are benefited only indirectly, and purely as the result of the genuinely independent and private choices of aid recipients."

The Ohio Court of Appeals reversed the ruling in 1997, but its ruling was overturned by the state supreme court. In the meantime, the general assembly had passed yet another bill to assist voucher and charter school students. This legislation directed the Cleveland School District to provide transportation for voucher and charter students to their schools of choice.

Inevitably, the matter went to the federal courts. In December 2000, the Court of Appeals for the Sixth Circuit ruled the Ohio program unconstitutional because government funding of private tuition promotes religious education. As the case moved toward the U.S. Supreme Court, it pitted Susan Tave Zelman, Ohio's superintendent of public instruction, who argued for the constitutionality of the vouchers, against Doris Simmons-Harris, the parent of a public school student. Several conservative and Religious Right organizations, including the Becket Fund for Religious Liberty and Pat Robertson's American Center for Law and Justice, filed amicus briefs in defense of school vouchers for religious schools.

The attorneys for both sides cited as precedent the 1947 Supreme Court ruling in *Everson v. Board of Education of Ewing Township*. In that case, a New Jersey school district had passed a plan allowing the use of public funds for the transportation of students to private schools. Arch R. Everson, a local taxpayer,

objected on the grounds that such payments violated the disestablishment clause of the First Amendment. A lower court ruled the
plan unconstitutional, but the New Jersey Court of Appeals over-
ruled that decision, and the case eventually found its way to the
U.S. Supreme Court. In a five-to-four decision, the Court upheld
the busing plan on the grounds that the program did not unduly
assist parochial schools, even though it might make parents more
likely to send their children to such schools.

Justice Hugo Black's majority opinion in the *Everson* case, however, also affirmed the notion of church-state separation, even as it
allowed for the transportation reimbursements. "No tax in any
amount, large or small, can be levied to support any religious activities or institutions, whatever they may be called, or whatever form
they may adopt to teach or practice religion," Black wrote. "Neither a state nor the Federal Government can, openly or secretly,
participate in the affairs of any religious organizations or groups
and vice versa. In the words of Jefferson, the clause against establishment of religion by law was intended to erect 'a wall of separation between Church and State.'"

On June 27, 2002, however, writing for a narrow five-four majority in the Ohio case *Zelman v. Simmons-Harris*, William Rehnquist said that the Ohio law did not violate the First Amendment
because "the Ohio program is neutral in all respects toward religion." John Paul Stevens issued a vigorous dissent. "Whenever we
remove a brick from the wall that was designed to separate religion
and government," he wrote, "we increase the risk of religious strife
and weaken the foundation of our democracy."[3]

Justice David Souter was even more distressed by the majority
ruling in favor of vouchers for religious schools. He thought it

unconscionable for a citizen's taxes to support beliefs with which he disagreed. "Religious teaching at taxpayer expense simply cannot be cordoned from taxpayer politics, and every major religion currently espouses social positions that provoke intense opposition," Souter wrote. He cited as examples Roman Catholic opposition to the death penalty, "the religious Zionism taught in many religious Jewish schools," or the "differential treatment of the sexes" espoused by Muslims and by Southern Baptists. "Views like these, and innumerable others, have been safe in the sectarian pulpits and classrooms of this Nation not only because the Free Exercise Clause protects them directly, but because the ban on supporting religious establishment has protected free exercise, by keeping it relatively private," Souter continued. "With the arrival of vouchers in religious schools, that privacy will go, and along with it will go confidence that religious disagreement will stay moderate."

But Souter also feared the corrosive effects of public money on religious organizations. "When government aid goes up, so does reliance on it; the only thing likely to go down is independence," Souter warned. "A day will come when religious schools will learn what political leverage can do, just as Ohio's politicians are now getting a lesson in the leverage exercised by religion." The dissenting justice wanted to "save religion from its own corruption."

According to its promotional materials, the mission of West Park Lutheran School is "to lead our children to know and respond to Jesus Christ as their Lord and Savior while providing academic excellence." No one disputes the school's right to do that. Nor, so far as I know, does anyone dispute the right of parents to send their students to religious schools. But should taxpayer money be subsidizing religiously sectarian instruction? The state of Ohio clearly thinks so, and five justices on the U.S. Supreme Court agreed.

On the face of it, the advocates for school vouchers have a good case. Public schools are in trouble in Cleveland and in many other parts of the country, and parents are increasingly uneasy about sending their children to them, especially as they approach junior and senior high school. Why shouldn't parents have the option of enrolling their children, at public expense, in schools the parents deem most appropriate?

This is the central argument behind the school-voucher initiative, and, at first blush, the logic is compelling. We allow for choice in the marketplace, after all, which has generally led to more and better options, as manufacturers and service industries compete with one another for customers. So, too, schools would compete with one another for students, and this "free marketplace" would force public schools to do a better job and to be more responsive to the needs of children.

I have no objection, at least in theory, to parents' sending their children to private schools or even to educating them at home. That freedom is fundamental. Some parents, for various reasons, have opted out of the public school system and send their children to private schools, religious or otherwise. They have every right to do so—but at their own expense.

Make no mistake about it: What lies behind most of the rhetoric about school vouchers is the desire to garner taxpayer support for sectarian education. According to a 2001 study by Policy Matters Ohio, a nonprofit research institute, 99.4 percent of Cleveland's voucher students were enrolled in religious schools, most of them Catholic, but also places like West Park Lutheran School.

But still another constituency wants to divert tax money from public schools, namely, the affluent, many of whom already send their children to private schools and would welcome a subsidy from public funds. The confluence of interest between economically prosperous citizens and the supporters of religious education has the makings of a powerful coalition. The "school choice" movement represents the alignment of the nation's wealthy with religious constituencies; although they may disagree on other issues, they have a mutual interest in seeing the vouchers succeed.

The results in Ohio bear this out. One-third of the students who use the school-voucher program in Ohio had parents who were wealthy enough to afford private education for their children before the voucher plan was implemented. According to Policy Matters Ohio, the nonprofit research institute, 33 percent of the students accepting vouchers five years into the "school choice" experiment were already enrolled in private schools. "The numbers suggest that vouchers in Cleveland are serving more as a subsidy for students already attending private schools," the report concluded, "than as an 'escape hatch' for students eager to leave the public schools."[4]

But these facts do not deter proponents of the voucher system, who insist on defending the program with specious arguments about social justice. Brennan and the so-called "school choice" advocates characterize themselves as defenders of the poor. "Every single one of us recognizes that if we don't solve the education dilemma in this society, the poorest among us will remain that way," he told the *Columbus Dispatch* in 2005. "And I will say with great sincerity, that is what drives me and the whole school-choice movement." Vouchers, advocates contend, will provide equal opportunity for children of all socioeconomic backgrounds. Voucher in hand, the argument goes, even the poorest children will be able to attend the best schools.[5]

That argument collapses, however, on closer examination. Take, for example, the failed ballot initiative in California several years ago, which would have provided every child with a voucher in the amount of $4,000. Tuition at the private Harvard-Westlake School in southern California was $22,700 for the 2005–2006 academic year, and the Castilleja School in Palo Alto charged $25,545. Or, to choose another venue, the last time I checked private day-school costs in New York City, the annual tuition was rapidly approaching $30,000. Do the school-voucher advocates really believe that a single mother working for minimum wage will come up with the additional $20,000 or more to enroll her child at Collegiate Prep School? For those less fortunate, the numbers wouldn't compute even if the amount of the $4,000 vouchers were doubled. Vouchers might work just fine for Silicon Valley millionaires or Goldman-Sachs households—and who would be inclined to turn down a $4,000 handout to be applied toward an elite education?—but the poorest children would be left behind. It occurs to me that one way to test the sincerity of those arguing for school vouchers on the basis of social justice would be to limit vouchers to children in households earning, say, less than $35,000. Would these advocates still be willing to expend all this energy to torture the Constitution if the only beneficiaries were indeed those less privileged?

Once again, the "school choice" experiment in Ohio confirms these suspicions. According to the same study by Policy Matters Ohio, the 21 percent of public school students who transferred to private schools using vouchers "were more likely to transfer out of a high-performing public school, a magnet school, or a school with test scores better than the district average." The voucher system, then, either removed students who were already attending elite public schools or siphoned the top students out of weaker schools, that is, out of classrooms like Dolly Goodwin's sixth grade at Walton School.

The charter schools, on the other hand, are thriving—economically, at least. The conservative economist Milton Friedman, who began advocating school choice in 1955, rhapsodized four decades later about the economic dividends that entrepreneurs could harvest from this scheme of diverting public money to private education. Writing in the *Washington Post* in 1995, Friedman, an avid proponent of laissez-faire capitalism, criticized "so-called public schools, which are really not public at all but simply private fiefs primarily of the administrators and the union officials." Although he stopped just short of calling for an end to what he referred to as "government schools," Friedman advocated massive and far-reaching voucher programs, adding that "the privatization of schooling would produce a new, highly active and profitable private industry."[6]

Brennan has proven him correct. During the 2004–2005 school year, according to the *Columbus Dispatch*, the state of Ohio shelled out $430 million for 63,500 students to attend charter schools around the state. An entity called White Hat Management, Brennan's umbrella corporation for thirty-one charter schools, collected $109 million, more than one-quarter of that total.[7]

And how are those charter schools faring? Out of the twenty-two of Brennan's schools subject to rating in 2004, the Ohio Department of Education placed eighteen in the categories of "academic

watch" or "academic emergency" because of poor student performance. Brennan defends the performance of his schools because so
many of the students, he claims, would otherwise have become
dropouts. He and other charter school advocates have also persuaded lawmakers in Ohio to relax their oversight of charter
schools.[8]

My experience in public schools, kindergarten through high
school, in Minnesota, Michigan, and Iowa suggests that education
is anything but an "industry," to use Friedman's term. Nor should
it be entrusted to entrepreneurs, who ultimately have interests beyond the education of children. With few exceptions, my teachers
were dedicated women and men who labored long hours for paltry
wages. Public school is where I learned the proverbial "three Rs,"
and I owe whatever writing ability I have to my eighth-grade
English teacher, Mrs. Helen Hier, who taught me the rudiments of
grammar and how to diagram sentences. But public schools also
taught me about people different from myself—Catholics and Jews
and African Americans, the children of Mexican workers, and
even, in the early 1970s, a few Bohemians—lessons I learned not
merely from textbooks but from daily interactions in the classroom
and on the playground.

My parents were not affluent by any stretch of the imagination,
so my experience cannot be attributed to residence in wealthy
neighborhoods or privileged school districts. But I was surely privileged in other ways—in my encounter with ideas and individuals
outside of my own insular world.

The self-styled "school choice" advocates would destroy all
that. Their use of public funds would support religious and charter

schools, both of which (unlike public schools) can choose whom they want to educate. "School choice" would also abet the stratification of education by subsidizing the tuition that wealthier Americans are already paying to elite private schools.

How does the Religious Right figure into all of this? The national debate surrounding voucher programs is just one aspect of a broader religious war on public education. Although most evangelicals were mired in their own subculture in the early 1960s, the Supreme Court caught their attention with two important rulings. In 1963, the case *Abington Township School District v. Schempp* came before the Court. Edward Schempp, a Unitarian, filed suit against his Pennsylvania township for requiring his children to read the Bible as part of their public education. At the first District Court trial, Schempp and his children testified that a literal reading of the Bible suggested specific religious doctrines "which were contrary to the religious beliefs which they held and to their familial teaching."

The Supreme Court took the *Schempp* case as an opportunity to clarify its deeply controversial decision the previous year in *Engel v. Vitale*. In that case, a group of parents in New York State had protested the requirement that their children recite at the beginning of each school day the following prayer: "Almighty God, we acknowledge our dependence upon Thee, and we beg Thy blessing upon us, our parents, our teachers and our Country." The Court ruled decisively on behalf of the parents: "We think that by using its public school system to encourage recitation of the Regents' prayer, the State of New York has adopted a practice wholly inconsistent with the Establishment Clause."

When *Schempp* came before the Court the following year, the Court once again ruled decisively against prescribed prayers in public school. Justice Tom C. Clark wrote on behalf of the Court: "We repeat and again reaffirm that neither a State nor the Federal Government can constitutionally force a person 'to profess a belief or disbelief in any religion.'"

Evangelical Christians responded to these twin rulings with something between disbelief and outrage, but they confined their responses primarily to setting up alternative, "Christian" schools. Jerry Falwell, for instance, announced plans in November 1966 for the formation of Lynchburg Christian Academy, ostensibly to counteract the effects of the *Engel* and *Schempp* decisions, but also, apparently, to evade a state-mandated program designed to accelerate the pace of racial integration in Virginia schools.[9]

By the 1980s, the war on "secular" education had become central to the mission of the Religious Right. Public education became one of its favorite whipping boys, responsible for everything from the secularization of society to juvenile incorrigibility. "I believe that the decay in our public school system suffered an enormous acceleration when prayer and Bible reading were taken out of the classroom by our U.S. Supreme Court," Falwell declared in 1980.[10]

Falwell had, of course, flagrantly distorted the meaning of the *Schempp* decision, as was the norm among Religious Right activists. The Court has never said that students cannot pray or read the Bible in public schools; it simply—and properly—prohibited school officials from organizing or leading prayers and devotional Bible reading in the public schools. As Clark wrote in the *Schempp* decision, "Nothing we have said here indicates that such study of the Bible or of religion, when presented objectively as part of a secular program of education, may not be effected consistently with the First Amendment."

Most evangelicals, in fact, have traditionally taken a jaundiced view of prescribed prayers, preferring spontaneous and extemporary prayer as representing a more authentic spirituality. In the New Testament, Jesus criticized those who made prayer into a spectator sport, "standing in the synagogues and on the street corners to be seen by others." He called them hypocrites, and he enjoined his followers instead, "go into your room, close the door and pray to your Father." Many evangelicals throughout American history have refused even to recite the Lord's Prayer, eschewing it as formalistic and, therefore, insincere.[11]

For that reason, the flap over prescribed, formal prayer in schools seems misplaced at least, even disingenuous. Why would evangelical parents want their children—who were (and are) perfectly free to pray silently in school, just as Jesus instructed—to recite a prayer mandated by school officials? Why would evangelical parents want to entrust catechetical instruction to public school officials? It's difficult, on the face of it, to understand what the fuss was all about. As Justice Hugo Black noted in the *Engel* case in 1962, "A union of government and religion tends to destroy government and degrade religion."[12]

Frustrated in their attempts to reinstate religious exercise in public schools, some leaders of the Religious Right began to herald the importance of religious schools. "Christian schools are the only hopes of training young men and young women who will be capable of taking the helm of leadership in every level of society," Falwell wrote in 1980. "It is the Christian school movement and the restoration of voluntary prayer in public schools that will provide the most important means of educating our children in the concepts of patriotism and morality."[13]

For many evangelicals, responding to the litany of complaints from the Religious Right, public schools no longer seemed tenable. On the eve of the first 1988 presidential primary, I spoke to a young couple in New Hampshire. "We're not going to send our kids into the snake pit of the public schools," the father hissed. "The whole curriculum is designed to turn children against their parents." They chose instead to educate their children at home.[14]

Aside from religious schools and (where available) charter schools, many evangelicals have turned to homeschooling in an effort to flee public education. In 2003, about 1.1 million children (up 29 percent from 850,000 in 1999) were educated at home in the United States, and 72 percent of parents who homeschool their children list "the desire to provide religious or moral instruction" as one of the factors in their decision. Lawree and Scott MacDonald of Antioch, California, for instance, pulled their teenage daughter out of public school late in 2001. The home environment, the mother told *Christianity Today*, is "safer both morally and socially."[15]

The drumbeat of criticism emanating from the leaders of the Religious Right has also convinced many evangelicals of the dangers of public education; many have even grown suspicious of the one virtue that has always been the key to the success and the longevity of America's experiment in pluralism: toleration. Leaders of the Religious Right have expressed their disdain for toleration and for pluralism itself, but none rivals James Dobson, head of Focus on the Family.

Dobson's comments about toleration and public education sparked a brief conflagration in 2002. In his March 28 radio broadcast, he said, "In the state of California, if I had a child there, I wouldn't put the youngster in a public school." Dobson objected to what he described as "homosexual propaganda" that children were allegedly being subjected to in public schools; the issue, in fact, was an initiative in California to teach schoolchildren tolerance of others. "I think it's time to get our kids out," Dobson declared.

Dobson's statement attracted a flurry of attention in both evangelical and neoconservative circles. Several months later, according to *Christianity Today*, Dobson reiterated his warning that "this godless and immoral curriculum and influence in the public schools is gaining momentum across the nation in ways that were unheard of just one year ago." He expanded his condemnation beyond California to the states of Connecticut, Massachusetts, Minnesota, New Jersey, Washington, Wisconsin, and Vermont, and to Washington, D.C., all of which he criticized for their "safe schools" laws that prohibit discrimination against homosexuals.[16]

Dobson's statements were immediately applauded by conservatives who had been pushing for the end of what they derisively call "government schools." Marshall Fritz, head of the Alliance for the Separation of School and State, with offices in Fresno, California, issued a statement: "With today's courageous and insightful statement, Dr. Dobson joins the millions of Americans who have already discovered that the public schools have become government indoctrination centers which are no place to train new generations of freedom loving Americans." Michael Farris, general counsel of the Home School Legal Defense Association and president of Patrick Henry College, chimed in: "Jim Dobson has always been a leader with courage and those who take a courageous stand on an issue need encouragement." Laura Schlessinger, a conservative talk-radio psychologist, also declared her agreement. "I stand with Dr. James Dobson," she said several days later.[17]

The Heritage Foundation, a conservative think tank that pushes for taxpayer-funded school vouchers and charter schools, including those run by religious groups, argues that the "battle over who should control America's schools is a battle for the future of our nation." On this point, at least, the Heritage Foundation is absolutely right. Throughout American history, public schools have played a formative role in American society. Following the English Conquest of New Netherland in 1664, for example, the Church of England established an English-speaking school, Trinity School, in New York City to compete with the Dutch school. So effective was Trinity School in altering the ethos of the colony that by the middle of the eighteenth century, Dutch church officials appealed to the Netherlands for an English-speaking minister; the younger generation could no longer understand Dutch.[18]

As public, or "common," schools took hold in the early decades of the nineteenth century, they became vehicles for social and economic equality, as well as for the inculcation of morality and the virtues of citizenship in the new nation. Protestant religious leaders recognized the importance of these schools. In Kentucky, for instance, the first three state education superintendents were ministers. Sheldon Jackson, a Presbyterian missionary, served as the first general agent for education in Alaska, and Samuel Lewis, Methodist lay minister, filled a similar post in Ohio. Another Presbyterian minister, William Holmes McGuffey, who was also a professor at Miami University in Ohio, compiled a series of graded readers, known as *Eclectic Readers*, which taught generations of schoolchildren religious, ethical, and moral principles.

Public schools have played an invaluable role by providing a common ground for children of different ethnic groups and religious persuasions, regardless of social class. In a pluralistic society, public schools provide an opportunity to explore differences and form friendships. At school, children interact with one another and, in the best of all worlds, learn to understand one another and to tolerate one another. Whatever common culture we have attained in this country has come about largely through the agency of public education. At the risk of sounding mawkish, I truly believe that public schools served to make America what it is by helping us forge a mutual understanding of one another as Americans.

Homeschooling, school vouchers, and charter schools all diminish the possibilities for such understanding. The private and specialized schools envisioned by the advocates of school vouchers and charter schools threaten that heritage and strike at the heart of the formative mechanism essential for the function of citizenship. By siphoning students from the public schools, private education inevitably narrows that meeting ground.

It also contributes to a ghetto mentality—socially, intellectually, and culturally. The creation of religious schools leads to heightened segregation of different racial and socioeconomic groups. The so-called "school choice" initiative is both a civil rights and a social justice issue, and real Christians, those who take seriously the teachings of Jesus, should be fighting against voucher programs and charter schools because they perpetuate divisions, rather than reconciliation, within society.

Indeed, the overwhelming irony surrounding the school-voucher movement is that it purports to be a conservative movement, and it certainly enjoys the support of many political, religious, and cultural conservatives. Yet, the balkanization that follows from the implementation of school vouchers and the formation of charter schools essentially ratifies the most sinister effects of postmodernism and deconstruction by dividing American society into religious, ethnic, economic, and special-interest groups, thereby tearing the fabric of American culture and identity.

I don't deny that reform is needed in America's public schools. Violence is rampant, and academic achievement has declined. Children have ever-shrinking attention spans in the age of television and video games. School administrators contend with balky unions; teachers face recalcitrant bureaucracies, and many of the most talented ones finally give up and pursue other, more lucrative careers.

The Bush administration's "No Child Left Behind Act" merely exacerbates the crisis of public education. The emphasis on standardized testing virtually compels teachers to "teach to the test," which, as any educator knows, is a pedagogical strategy utterly inimical to learning. An even more cynical reading of the bill, one advanced by Jonathan Kozol, an educational expert and a former public school teacher, is that the legislation was designed to accelerate the demise of public education. "The kind of testing we are doing today is sociopathic in its repetitive and punitive nature," he told the *New York Times Magazine* in 2005. "Its driving motive is to highlight failure in inner-city schools as dramatically as possible in order to create a ground swell of support for private vouchers or other privatizing schemes." It's quite possible that what Kozol describes is an unintended consequence of "No

Child Left Behind," but the deleterious effects of the bill cannot be ignored.[19]

The collusion of business interests and the interests of the Religious Right on the matter of public education should make us suspicious. In the end, the war on public education is about money—the huge opportunities for profiting from parents' fears of secular education. In its war against public education, the Religious Right has allied itself with affluent Americans already paying for private education and with antigovernment, free-market conservatives who support vouchers and charter schools for very different reasons, to advance their own political and economic agendas.

But this thinking is shortsighted, and it abandons the crucial task of intellectual and social formation to capitalists. In an address before the convention of the National Association for the Advancement of Colored People in 1999, Reg Weaver, an African American and vice president of the National Education Association, pointed out the obvious: If capitalists are supporting school vouchers, the scheme is probably not calibrated to the best interests of education. "If most minority children, children of color, children of disadvantage and poverty, are going to have any chance at a quality education," Weaver said, "they aren't going to get it from big business, they aren't going to get it from the tender mercies of the free market, and they sure aren't going to get it from the scheme cooked up by the far right. They can, however, get it from a reformed and revitalized—a redeemed—public education system."[20]

The future of American democracy hangs in the balance in the tussle over homeschooling, school vouchers, and public education. The large and growing movement toward private education and homeschooling represents a betrayal of an essential component of

American culture, and I find it paradoxical that the very people who purport to reclaim America's past are the same people seeking to jettison such a key and formative institution in America's history. Public education, and the underlying conviction that schools are important gathering places, is central to our identity as Americans; public schools provide the most logical place, perhaps the only place, where future generations, especially within a pluralistic context, can coexist with at least a measure of comity and learn the rudiments of democracy. Whatever their shortcomings—and I don't want to understate those shortcomings—public schools can and must be preserved. If we care anything about democracy, we must care a great deal about public education.

In the face of overwhelming deficiencies in public education, school vouchers and charter schools sound like a quick fix. They rescue us from the hard work and the difficult choices required to reclaim the proud and distinguished legacy of public education in America. But school vouchers are chimerical, especially in an age where we face, more directly than ever before in our history, the challenges of pluralism. Now is not the time to encourage the balkanization of our schools and, by extension, our society.

The school voucher discussion will not abate soon. The Supreme Court's unfortunate five-to-four decision in 2002 to approve the voucher plan in Cleveland handed the enemies of disestablishment the victory they had long sought. The issue is now in the hands of state legislators, who must make the appropriations for school vouchers and the provisions for charter schools. Still, those who value the First Amendment and public education cannot afford to be complacent, in part because the voucher proposal has the potential to unite two constituencies into a powerful coalition:

religious conservatives, on the one hand, and those who already send their children to nonreligious private schools, on the other. The appeal for the former group is obvious: Why not have your religious convictions supported financially by the government, even if this threatens the First Amendment proscription against established religion?

The latter group finds vouchers attractive because they would offset the expensive tuition costs they are already paying for private schooling, as the experience in Ohio demonstrates. These people, by and large, are more affluent and can afford these tuitions, so why should the government subsidize them, especially when that money could be helping to educate those less privileged? If the neoconservatives and the Religious Right have their way, "government schools" will disappear altogether, and learning will take place in the home, in voucher schools run by religious groups, or in charter schools operated by capitalists.

I can't imagine anything less democratic.

Patrick Henry College provides a further example of how some evangelicals propose to extend the protective cocoon of the subculture beyond the home and beyond religious schools to the collegiate level. The people at Patrick Henry College aspire, in turn, to run the nation.

Located in Purcellville, Virginia, where the foothills of the Blue Ridge Mountains meet the western edge of Washington, D.C.'s suburban sprawl, Patrick Henry is the West Point of the Religious Right. This is a college like none other. Founded in 2000 by Michael Farris, and funded by such moguls of the Religious Right as Beverly and Tim LaHaye (author of the *Left Behind* series),

Patrick Henry College unabashedly mixes biblical Christianity with American patriotism. The school states that its mission is "to train Christian men and women who will lead our nation and shape our culture with timeless biblical values and fidelity to the spirit of the American founding."[21]

Portraits of Patrick Henry, George Washington, Theodore Roosevelt, and (somewhat improbably, given his dim view of organized religion) Benjamin Franklin bedeck the walls of Founders Hall, the central building at Patrick Henry College. The bulletin board of the library in the basement announced several new acquisitions: *Let Us Pray: A Plea for Prayer in Our Schools*; *Global Warming and Other Eco-Myths*; and *The Shadow University: The Betrayal of Liberty on America's Campuses*. The newspaper of choice on the campus of Patrick Henry College is the conservative *Washington Times*, not the *Washington Post*. Founders Hall and the satellite dormitories are all built in a faux-colonial style similar to the architecture favored by large Southern Baptist congregations.

The overwhelming majority of the school's two-hundred-plus students were homeschooled in conservative households. Many seem determinedly—or obliviously—out of fashion; their dress tends in the direction of khakis and white shirts instead of jeans and T-shirts, or skirts and purses rather than midriffs and backpacks. Students pepper their speech with phrases like, "That's awesome!" A sign on the door of the fitness room reads, "Separate times for men and women are available upon request." In contrast to other campuses, the drug of choice here is caffeine, and even at dawn on a wintry December morning, students filed into the student center to prepare for their eight o'clock classes.

I met a student named Daniel Burns Jr. on that morning, just as the sun poked over the horizon. Burns, seated behind the security desk in Founders Hall, was educated at home by his parents in Bridgeville, Pennsylvania. A major in government and public policy and a member of the moot court team, Burns plans to attend law school and then work for some sort of public-service group, such as the Home School Legal Defense Association or Pat Robertson's American Center for Law and Justice, founded by the televangelist in 1990 explicitly to counter the efforts of the American Civil Liberties Union.

Burns, twenty-one years old, could also fall back on a career in public relations because when I asked him about Patrick Henry College, he waxed rhapsodic. "I love it here," he said. "It's the right place for me." He ticked off the distinctive characteristics of the school. Patrick Henry, he said, seeks "to lead the nation and shape the culture." Faculty and students were "helping to reform the culture back to how the founders intended it to be, shaped around the ideals of limited government and personal freedom." This approach, Burns added, "is informed by our Christian faith." He paused. "We want to take those ideals and principles and restore them to our government."

I asked Burns for directions to an eight o'clock course called "Principles of Biblical Reasoning." There, I found students seated neatly in rows, prepared to supply answers as the instructor guided them through Augustine and Aquinas. "Is morality discovered, or is morality created?" he asked. "The secondary principles of morality are created," one student replied, "whereas the first principles are ingrained or written on our heart."

Both for teacher and students, this discussion of the natural law tradition represented far more than simply an intellectual exercise. "Human law is an extension or a particularization of natural law," the instructor insisted; natural law, therefore, was inviolable. The consequence of abandoning the immutability of natural law, according to the instructor, was what he called "postmodern hermeneutics," which he characterized as, "If you don't like it, change it." This was the besetting sin of modern liberalism, he said. "If we find certain elements of morality distasteful," he continued with his caricature, "we simply change them."

These comments clearly resonated with students eager to advance their conservative views in the public arena. "I was thinking of this yesterday at the Supreme Court," one man volunteered, "all these ladies marching around with posters supporting abortion." The instructor agreed. "Christians by and large understand that liberty is a very important thing," he said, but he avoided the conundrum implicit in that statement: How can someone who affirms personal liberty as a fundamental right guaranteed (presumably) by natural law support measures that would deny that liberty to a pregnant woman and insist that the state regulate gestation? Nor was it at all clear how that comported with the school's professed ideals of "limited government and personal freedom."

Michael Farris, the college's founding president and an attorney, teaches a course on constitutional law. The class is organized around an analysis of Supreme Court rulings, with Farris offering a kind of good-natured commentary. "What the environmental movement wants to do in this country," he offered, "is they want to turn other people's property into parks without paying for it." Farris, an ordained Baptist minister and the Republican nominee for lieutenant governor of Virginia in 1992, was unstinting in his criticism of individual Supreme Court justices, providing a kind of running tally of which justices needed to be replaced in order for particular decisions to be overturned. Commenting on what he regarded as a tilt toward the left on the part of Anthony Kennedy, a Reagan appointee, for example, Farris said, "I think Kennedy is going through what the left calls growth." Kennedy's problem, according to Farris, was "just hanging around with the wrong crowd." As for John Paul Stevens, the oldest justice, Farris cracked that "he was appointed, I think, by Franklin Pierce."[22]

Farris, who together with his wife educated their own ten children at home, became an activist on behalf of homeschool families in 1983 when he founded the Home School Legal Defense Association. The organization, which now claims to represent eighty-one thousand families, each of which pays about $100 annually in dues, exists "to protect and advance the liberty of parents to educate their children at home." The organization also fights to exempt homeschool parents from most state educational regulations, including the requirement that parents have college or high school diplomas or that they submit to certification tests. Farris, who once referred to the public school system as a "godless monstrosity," believes that the attempts on the part of various states to quash homeschooling turned out to be a boon for the Religious Right. "It just encouraged a whole lot of people to get involved politically," he said. "That's good."

Patrick Henry College evolved out of Farris's commitment to homeschooling. As more and more homeschool parents expressed uneasiness with sending their homeschooled children to secular colleges and universities, Farris came up with the idea of a college catering principally to homeschoolers. The curriculum here reinforces the religiously and politically conservative curricula that many parents taught at home. "Any biology, Bible or other courses at PHC dealing with creation will teach creation from the understanding of Scripture that God's creative work, as described in Genesis 1:1–31, was completed in six twenty-four hour days," the school's website assures parents. "In this context, PHC in particular expects its biology faculty to provide a full exposition of the claims of the theory of Darwinian evolution, intelligent design and other major theories while, in the end, teach creation as both biblically true and as the best fit to observed data." Students who attend Patrick Henry College, moreover, pledge to "reserve sexual activity for the sanctity of marriage" and promise to "seek and obtain parental permission when pursuing a romantic relationship."

In founding the college, Farris was not content simply to provide a sheltered environment for evangelical adolescents. He sought to prepare them to reshape the nation. Farris chose Purcellville as the site for the college for a strategic reason: Only fifty miles outside of Washington, D.C., its location offered students the opportunity to use their education to influence public policy in a decidedly conservative direction. "The most common thing I hear is parents telling me they want their kids to be on the Supreme Court," Farris told the *New York Times*. "And if we put enough kids in the farm system, some may get to the major leagues."[23]

On the Thursday of my visit, the daily chapel was decentralized; students met in the lounge of their dormitories with other members of their residence halls rather than in a plenary session. A large sign in the lobby of Red Hill dormitory read, "No Eating Drinking or

Smoking." A man who had introduced himself to me as Jonathan, the resident assistant, asked one of the residents to open the gathering with a prayer. He then offered some thoughts of his own. "I was praying through some stuff over Thanksgiving break," he began. "It's been sort of a crazy, stressful semester—spiritually stressful. I just realized that without God's grace I can't handle this stuff." Residents, a few of whom had just rolled out of bed, were dressed in everything from pajamas and blankets to navy suits, white button-down shirts, and red ties. One man wore a T-shirt with "Republican Team" emblazoned across his chest. "We can't make it on our own," Jonathan continued, almost plaintively. "We can't live up to everyone else's expectations." His auditors nodded in agreement.

The residents then echoed their resident adviser's sentiments. A man named Brian lamented his "moral weaknesses," and another noted that he had been "a lot more victorious over sin the last few days." The subject of stress among the students at Patrick Henry College elicited a good deal of comment. "Part of the problem is, I don't think we in the student body are praying enough," one resident opined. "If God is going to do a work through this school, it has to be by his strength."

As the end of the chapel hour approached, Jonathan asked the residents to close in prayer. "Lord Jesus, we just come before you today," Jamie began. "Father God, we pray for class renewal," by which he presumably meant a renewal of piety. Another resident reminded the Almighty that "we have something truly different going on here" at Patrick Henry College, and still another intoned, "Thank you for what you are doing at this school, and in us individually."

Indeed, the administrators and the students at Patrick Henry have a sense that their school is a place of destiny and that they, as students, are called to great things. Aaron Carlson, a senior, describes the students (in a careening and, to say the least, perplexing metaphor) as "the shining tip of the spear in the vision of PHC." Craig Drinkall of McHenry, Illinois, told me that he appreciated the "Christian atmosphere" of Patrick Henry College. A sophomore majoring in public policy, Drinkall aspires to work in the foreign service. Kelsey Staples from Atlanta, Georgia, also a sophomore, is a strategic intelligence major. When I asked where she saw herself in ten years, she replied that she hoped to be involved in some aspect of government intelligence. "It'd be cool to work for the CIA or the NSA," she said.

"Our nation is in desperate need of a new generation of godly leadership," Farris wrote in a recent fund-raising letter. "Patrick Henry College is training an army of young people who will lead the nation and shape the culture with biblical values." Indeed, Patrick Henry College provides a conduit to nearby Washington, especially to the White House and to Capitol Hill; since 2002, twenty-four students have served as White House interns. Students also work as interns in the offices of Religious Right favorites in Congress, and Republican politicians return the favor by visiting campus or by showering the school with high praise. Rick Santorum of Pennsylvania, described by the college's promotional materials as "a courageous and articulate champion of the pro-life and the pro-family movement," visited campus to promote his book. His fellow Republican senator, Tom Coburn of Oklahoma, said of the college, "I'm just thankful that it's there. I want a blessing to be poured out on it. I want it to be extremely successful because our country needs Patrick Henry College."[24]

Having attended a college not all that dissimilar from Patrick Henry College, I understand the attractions of such a school. Indeed, evangelical colleges can be important places of transition from the evangelical subculture to the larger world, as mine was for me. When I arrived as a freshman at Trinity College in the North Shore suburbs of Chicago, I found there a group of young and intellectually energetic professors who were willing to challenge the presuppositions of their theologically, politically, and socially conservative students without trying at the same time to deprive them of their faith. The school was far from perfect, but it served for me as a kind of halfway house between the sectarianism of my childhood and the wider world. It provided a safe harbor for my tentative forays into the sea of pluralism and secularism; I was seldom beyond the reach of a life buoy in the hands of someone who was learning to navigate the same waters, someone seeking to remain faithful to his evangelical religious convictions while at the same time engaging the larger culture critically.

Patrick Henry College, I fear, offers no such challenges to the theologically and politically conservative ideas of its homeschooled students. Instead, it affirms, almost without exception, everything they have been taught since infancy, from creationism or intelligent design to biblical inerrancy and the Religious Right's shopworn narrative of the supposed Christian origins of the United States and its subsequent lapse into moral decay. The appeal of a place like Patrick Henry College for parents is obvious; their child will

never have to face serious challenges to his faith or her presuppositions, except for those rendered in caricature. How many Patrick
Henry students, I wonder, have read *The Origin of Species* or *The
Catcher in the Rye* or *Fast Food Nation* or *The Feminine Mystique*
or *Das Kapital* or *The Autobiography of Malcolm X*?

Such an environment quashes critical thought and intellectual engagement; instead, it produces ideologues, and ideologues, sadly, are
in great demand these days in a cultural and political environment
that thrives on a dualistic view of reality, one that divides the world
into neat categories of black and white, good and evil. This kind of
education, which is an extension of homeschooling or religious
schools, never encourages students to entertain seriously any ideas
that might threaten the shibboleths of their evangelical upbringing.

The perils of such an education immediately become clear
when one contemplates the school's stated intention of grooming
future political leaders. The many students who make the short
commute from Purcellville, Virginia, to Washington, D.C., may
never have encountered a compelling argument in favor of, say, religious pluralism or civil unions or evolution. They will have had
virtually no interaction with anyone outside of their religious and
demographic cohort—more than 90 percent of Patrick Henry students are white. The people who support and operate Patrick
Henry College expect the school's graduates to run America, a
nation that has been defined throughout its history by religious
and ethnic pluralism. But they are doing nothing to prepare their
graduates to grapple sincerely with America's greatest challenges.

As a parent, I understand very well the desire to cosset children in
the safety of the domestic sphere or within a subculture defined by

ethnic, religious, or economic homogeneity such as that offered by private or religious schools. (There is probably more than a little truth to the maxim that a neoconservative is a liberal with a teenage daughter.) For much of the twentieth century, evangelicals found comfort within their subculture as a place of refuge from the outside world, which they came increasingly to regard as both corrupt and corrupting. The homeschool movement and the impulse to send children to religious schools merely represent an extension of that fortress mentality.

I wonder, though, if that is what Jesus had in mind for his followers. "You are the salt of the earth," he said in the Sermon on the Mount. "You are the light of the world. A city on a hill cannot be hidden. Neither do people light a lamp and put it under a bowl. Instead they put it on its stand, and it gives light to everyone in the house." Somehow, education in a segregated context—religiously, racially, or economically—seems to diminish the possibility of throwing light on the remainder of society.[25]

And what about the effects of this segmentation on American society itself? For nearly two hundred years, public education has provided a laboratory for democracy. Common schools, beginning in the nineteenth century, took as their task the education of the public and the creation of an informed and responsible citizenry. Although public education has never fulfilled every ideal, schools have been a powerful engine for social change. They have provided a venue of common ground for students of different religious, ethnic, and socioeconomic backgrounds, a place where they might learn from their differences, celebrate their similarities, and find a way to live with one another in at least a measure of comity. In short, they learned the rudiments of democracy.

That is an ideal vision, I acknowledge, but what institution could possibly bear the burden of such outsized expectations? What I find remarkable about public education is its continuing success in the face of such relentless criticism as that leveled by neoconservatives and the Religious Right. The glass is half full, not half empty, and now is not the time to give up on the noble enterprise of public education. In a society that has always been characterized by pluralism, and is more so now than ever, we need public schools like never before if we mean to perpetuate this great experiment of American democracy. And, Mr. Dobson, why *shouldn't* schoolchildren learn to be tolerant of others, even those with a different sexual orientation?

No one disputes that public education is in trouble, especially in places like Cleveland, but the attempts on the part of the "school choice" advocates to accelerate, rather than to arrest, that decline are reprehensible and shortsighted. Before heeding the siren call of school vouchers and charter schools, herding our children into schools run by capitalists or religious sectarians at taxpayer expense, we as a society should assess seriously the real costs of giving up on public education, costs calculated not merely in dollars but in the future of democracy itself.

chapter 4

Creationism by Design

The Religious Right's Quest
for Intellectual Legitimacy

*Just because a lot of people make noise doesn't make
it an intellectual issue. Just because a lot of people
believe in astrology doesn't mean it's true. Just
because a lot of people think that there are aliens who
abduct people in spaceships doesn't make it true. It
would be bizarre to claim that the ability of a group
to gain a great deal of publicity for a viewpoint
constitutes its intellectual seriousness, otherwise any
form of demagoguery that gets a hearing would have
to be so honored.*
          —STEPHEN JAY GOULD, 1994

FOR THOSE WHO FEEL CALLED ON TO DEFEND the integrity of the
book of Genesis, the ordinary, garden-variety creationism of decades past is passé. Charles Darwin's *The Origin of Species* landed
in American bookstores on November 24, 1859, and the entire supply of 1,250 copies sold out by day's end. The onset of the Civil
War blunted somewhat the effects of Darwin's ideas as Americans
were preoccupied with the war and the fate of the republic, but by

the closing decades of the nineteenth century, American Protestants had begun to choose sides. Many Protestants saw no conflict in harmonizing the Genesis account of creation with new understandings of science. "Evolution is God's way of doing things," John Fiske, a philosopher who taught for a time at Harvard, wrote. Another approach was simply to acknowledge that the creation stories at the beginning of the Hebrew Bible were allegorical, not historical, that the stories were intended to convey something essential about the character of God, the nature of humanity, and the divine origins of all creation. The text itself never claimed to be history, much less science, these Protestants reasoned. The creation stories should be seen instead as part of the rich and edifying tradition of Hebrew literature.[1]

Some evangelicals, however, remained wary of Darwin's theory of evolution. Taken to their logical conclusion, of course, Darwin's ideas undermined evangelicals' traditional, literalist approach to the scriptures. If the Genesis account of creation could no longer be regarded as history, they reasoned, then the remainder of the Bible might also be suspect. Perched on the precipice of a slippery slope, many evangelicals resisted Darwin's evolutionary theory, first by asserting the literal, historical accuracy of Genesis, then through legislation, next by trying to discredit evolution itself, and, most recently, by trying to advance something called "intelligent design."

The most dramatic showdown between creationism and Darwinism occurred in July 1925 on the second story of the Rhea County courthouse in Dayton, Tennessee, during the famous Scopes trial. On January 21, 1925, a corn and tobacco farmer named John Washington Butler had introduced a bill that forbade the teaching of evolution in Tennessee public schools. Butler had run for state representative in 1922 on the promise to introduce such legislation, confident that ninety-nine out of a hundred of his constituents supported such a ban. He drafted the legislation, which made it "unlawful for any teacher" in state-supported schools "to teach any theory that denies the story of the Divine creation of man as taught in the Bible, and to teach instead that man has descended from a lower order of animals." Later, Butler reportedly said, "No, I didn't know anything about evolution when I introduced it. I'd read in the papers that boys and girls were coming home from school and telling their fathers and mother that the Bible was all nonsense."

Tennessee governor Austin Peay signed the bill into law because he needed the support of rural legislators, but he was confident that the law would not be enforced. "After a careful examination," he told reporters, "I can find nothing of consequence in the books now being taught in our schools with which this bill will interfere in the slightest manner. Therefore, it will not put our teachers in jeopardy. Probably the law will never be applied."

The American Civil Liberties Union, however, had other ideas. The organization placed advertisements in newspapers across the state seeking someone who might be willing to challenge the legitimacy of the Butler Act. A few local civic boosters in Dayton, a small, isolated hamlet of about eighteen hundred souls (down from three thousand in the 1890s) in the eastern part of the state, sensed an opportunity. They gathered at Fred Robinson's drugstore and eventually summoned a young teacher at Rhea County High School, a general science instructor and part-time football coach. Although John Thomas Scopes couldn't recall whether or not he had actually taught evolution when he filled in for the regular biology teacher, the boosters plied him with a fountain drink and secured his consent to test the validity of the law. They summoned the constable, who arrested the teacher and then immediately released him on bond, whereupon Scopes promptly slipped out of the drugstore for a game of tennis.[2]

The Butler Act had touched a nerve. Americans found themselves in the throes of change in the 1920s. Victorian America, with its prim orderliness, was giving way to the jazz age and the era of the flapper. A decade earlier, a group of conservative Protestants had published a series of pamphlets, *The Fundamentals*, in an attempt to stanch the drift toward theological liberalism, or "modernism," in Protestant denominations. These writers stoutly defended the integrity of the Bible against all attacks, including what they perceived as the threat of Darwinism. Fundamentalists had been agitating against the teaching of evolution in public schools; by 1925, they had succeeded in having such prohibitive legislation introduced in fifteen states. While the Butler Act was being considered in the Tennessee legislature, for example, Billy Sunday, a famous evangelist and former baseball player for the Chicago White Stockings, came to Memphis to rally support for the legislation.

The Scopes "monkey trial" itself unfolded amid a carnival atmosphere. Public interest in the trial was so intense that WGN, the clear-channel radio station in Chicago, carried the proceedings live. Partisans on both sides filled the courthouse square, and Dayton itself was bedecked with banners welcoming visitors and staking out positions on the merits of the case. Organ grinders and serpent handlers circulated through the crowds, much to the delight of the phalanx of journalists, led by the acerbic H. L. Mencken of the

Baltimore Sun. Mencken mercilessly lampooned the denizens of eastern Tennessee, but he took particular delight in criticizing the lead attorney for the prosecution, William Jennings Bryan, three-time Democratic nominee for president and Woodrow Wilson's secretary of state. Bryan's immediate opponent in the steamy Dayton courtroom, however, was his erstwhile friend and political ally, Clarence Darrow. Although Darrow and Bryan had been on the same side of many progressive causes in the decades surrounding the turn of the twentieth century, the Scopes trial cast them as adversaries: Darrow led the Scopes defense team, and Bryan, who had not practiced law for thirty years, assisted the prosecution.

The turning point of the trial occurred when Darrow persuaded Bryan himself to take the witness stand, with the understanding that Darrow would reciprocate later in the trial. Darrow peppered Bryan with a sequence of village atheist questions, which Bryan handled ineptly. "You have given considerable study to the Bible, haven't you, Mr. Bryan?" Darrow began. Bryan answered proudly that he had "studied the Bible for about fifty years." Darrow asked whether several biblical accounts—Jonah spending three days inside a whale, Noah and the great flood, Joshua making the sun stand still—should be taken literally. Bryan emphatically responded that "everything in the Bible should be accepted as it is given there."

When Darrow asked if the Genesis account of creation should be construed as seven twenty-four-hour days, however, Bryan backpedaled: "My impression is that they were periods." Darrow persisted, and Bryan became more flustered. When he declared, in response to another of Darrow's questions, "I do not think about things I don't think about," Darrow shot back, "Do you think about the things you do think about?" Finally, an exasperated Bryan accused Darrow of leveling a "slur at the Bible" and declared his intention to defend the scriptures against such attacks. "I object to your statement," Darrow replied angrily, and to "your fool ideas that no intelligent Christian on earth believes."

By then, however, the trial had careened out of control. Following the outburst between Darrow and Bryan, the judge adjourned the proceedings until the following morning, when he ruled that the preceding day's exchange should be stricken from the record. Darrow then asked that his client, John Scopes, be found guilty so that the matter could go to a higher court. The jury agreed. Although Scopes was convicted of violating the Butler Act and fined $100 (the conviction was later overturned by the Tennessee Supreme Court on a technicality), Bryan and, by extension, all evangelicals lost decisively in the larger courtroom of public opinion. The abrupt end to the trial had deprived Bryan of the opportunity to deliver his summation, which he had been preparing for weeks. He stayed in Dayton and died there six days after the trial.

"Let no one mistake it for comedy, farcical though it may be in all its details," Mencken wrote at the conclusion of the trial. "It serves notice on the country that Neanderthal man is organizing in these forlorn backwaters of the land, led by a fanatic, rid of sense and devoid of conscience." Mencken ridiculed "Bryan and his balderdash" and said that the three-time candidate for president "preferred the company of rustic ignoramuses." Mencken mourned "the punishment that falls upon a civilized man cast among fundamentalists" and expressed sympathy for the educated clergy of Tennessee, who were "tossing pathetically under the imbecilities of their evangelical colleagues."[3]

Evangelicals, chastened by the opprobrium leveled at them during and after the trial, retreated from the broader society after 1925 to construct their distinctive subculture as a place of refuge from the larger world. Still, they persisted in their battle against evolution and were remarkably successful at the state and local levels in blocking the teaching of evolution in public schools. Publishers, afraid of a backlash from evangelicals, quietly expunged evolution from their textbooks. In 1958, a year before the centennial of the publication of *The Origin of Species*, Hermann J. Muller, a Columbia-educated, Nobel Prize–winning geneticist, lamented the neglect of evolutionary theory in an address entitled "One Hundred Years without Darwinism Are Enough." Tennessee, to cite another example of the persistence of creationist sentiment, didn't repeal the Butler Act until 1967.[4]

The tide finally begun to turn against the creationists when the Soviet Union catapulted a tiny satellite named *Sputnik* into outer space on October 4, 1957. Suddenly, it became clear that the United States lagged dangerously in scientific knowledge and what quickly became known as the space race. John F. Kennedy announced a new science initiative early in his administration, along with the breathtaking goal of "landing a man on the moon and returning him safely to the earth" by the end of the 1960s. Evangelical and fundamentalist scruples about Darwinism were swept aside before the juggernaut of science education because, as scientists insisted with near unanimity, evolutionary theory provides the essential foundation for all scientific inquiry. Any scientists of the future must therefore be conversant with Darwin's ideas.[5]

Those who propagated a literal interpretation of the Genesis account of creation suddenly found themselves on the defensive.

They organized several societies in the 1960s and 1970s—the Creation Research Society, Bible Science Association, the Institute for Creation Research, among others—that advocated "creationism" and, later, "scientific creationism," a sometimes comic attempt to clothe biblical literalism with scientific legitimacy.

As evangelicals began to venture outside of their subculture in the 1970s, public education became one of their battlegrounds, in part because it nicely conjoined disaffection with the school-prayer decisions of the 1960s with abiding uneasiness over evolution. Mel and Norma Gabler, evangelicals from Longview, Texas, became pivotal and transitional figures in this new initiative. As early as 1961, they began to question some of the material in their teenage son's textbooks, material they found inaccurate, amoral, or both. Mel Gabler, who died in 2004, took early retirement as a clerk from the Humble Pipe Line Company in order to join his wife in vetting textbooks for the state—and then challenging objectionable material before the Texas State Board of Education.

In response to protests from the Gablers, the Texas Board of Education mandated in 1974 that any textbooks "which treat the subject of evolution substantively in explaining the historical origins of humankind shall be edited, if necessary, to clarify that the treatment is theoretical rather than factually verifiable." Because Texas has a statewide textbook adoption policy (rather than leaving the matter to local school boards), the effects of the 1974 rule, as well as of others since, have rippled far beyond Texas. Publishers, eager to tap into such a large market, have generally shied away from any mention of evolution.

Opposition to the Gablers recalls the invective that Mencken heaped upon Bryan at the Scopes trial. Molly Ivins, a nationally syndicated columnist from Texas, once characterized the couple from Longview as "two ignorant, fear-mongering, right-wing fruit-loops who have spent the last twenty years doing untold damage to public education in this state." The Gablers, of course, saw things differently. "Why shouldn't we fight?" Norma asked rhetorically. "It's our children, our tax money, and our government. And it's our rights that are being violated. If textbooks can't teach Christian principles, then they shouldn't teach against Christianity."[6]

Aside from efforts to reintroduce public prayer in the schools, the Religious Right, following the lead of the Gablers, decided once again to engage the battle against Darwinism in public schools. Most of the skirmishes between scientists and the Religious Right, however, took place in local school districts. In Vista, California, for instance, voters elected a fundamentalist majority to the local board of education in November 1992, including John Tyndall, who worked for the Institute for Creation Research in nearby Santee. Although he had disavowed any intention of introducing scientific creationism into the public school curriculum, Tyndall, as part of the majority coalition, voted to require the use of a textbook entitled *Of Pandas and People*, a kind of creationist classic propagating scientific creationism, in Vista schools. Teachers resisted, the California Education Association protested, and the public finally mobilized by recalling Tyndall and one of his conservative allies, Joyce Lee, from the board in November 1994.

Since Vista, communities across the country have divided over the teaching of creationism in public schools. Most scientists scoff at the science behind "scientific creationism," dismissing as preposterous creationist claims that the Grand Canyon, for example, was formed in a matter of weeks. Creationists, such as Duane Gish, counter by

protesting that research programs like his Institute for Creation Research don't have access to the federal funds that would allow them to
undertake massive research to validate their claims.

Indeed, the legal history of cases addressing the evolution-
creationism controversy is extensive and benumbingly consistent,
but the multiplicity of cases suggests the variety of ways in which
conservatives have sought to insinuate creationism into public education. Courts have repeatedly refused to countenance creationism
as anything but religious and therefore impermissible in public
schools because it violates the establishment clause of the First
Amendment. In 1968, in *Epperson v. Arkansas*, the U.S. Supreme
Court struck down as unconstitutional a state law, modeled on Tennessee's Butler Act, that prohibited the teaching of evolution in public schools. The First Amendment to the U.S. Constitution, the
court ruled, does not allow a state to require that teaching and learning be tailored to fit the religious convictions of any particular group.

Twelve years later, however, the state of Arkansas was back in
U.S. District Court to defend its "balanced treatment" law, which
required that equal play be given to both "evolution-science" and
"creation-science." In the *McLean v. Arkansas Board of Education*
ruling, the court again struck down the law, arguing that "creation-
science" is religion because it is not in fact science and that the
theory of evolution does not presuppose either the existence or the
absence of a creator.[7]

A Supreme Court ruling in 1987 that creationism was a religious belief, not science, and therefore could not be taught in public schools, should have put the matter finally to rest. Louisiana's
"Creationism Act" forbade the teaching of evolution unless it was

taught alongside "creation science." The Court's decision in this case, *Edwards v. Aguillard*, held that, with its belief that a supernatural being lay behind the creation process, creationism was in fact a religion and that its teaching in the context of a public school classroom represented an infringement of the First Amendment's establishment clause.

And on and on. The Seventh Circuit Court of Appeals ruled in 1990 that a school district may prohibit a school teacher from teaching creation science without violating the teacher's right to free speech since creationism is a religious ideology. The decision in *Peloza v. Capistrano School District*, issued by the Ninth Circuit Court of Appeals in 1994, rejected the creationist argument that evolution was a religion and that a school district's refusal to teach creationism violated a student's First Amendment right to free exercise of religion. In *Freiler v. Tangipahoa Parish Board of Education*, decided in U.S. District Court and affirmed by the Fifth Circuit Court of Appeals in 1999, the courts rejected a policy requiring teachers to read a disclaimer whenever they taught evolution, ostensibly so that the schools would promote "critical thinking." The court noted that evolution was the only subject singled out for such treatment and that "the School Board is endorsing religion by disclaiming the teaching of evolution in such a manner as to convey the message that evolution is a religious viewpoint."

Despite this record of legal setbacks, however, conservatives seeking to legitimate creationism as science have persisted. Like kudzu or like Jason in *Friday the Thirteenth*, creationism refuses to die. The Religious Right manages to keep the issue alive by inventing new guises for the Genesis account of creation, versions or approaches that they hope will finally pass muster with the courts and allow creationists to propagate their theology in public schoolrooms.

Despite these ongoing legal battles, the debate over origins itself remained fairly stagnant until the early 1990s. Creationists hankered after scientific legitimacy, while the scientific community systematically debunked the scientific pretensions of the creationists. The entrance of a most unlikely voice into the debate, that of Phillip E. Johnson, a professor at Boalt Hall, the law school of the University of California, Berkeley, altered the equation. Johnson, a graduate of Harvard and the University of Chicago, had clerked for Earl Warren, chief justice of the U.S. Supreme Court, and was enjoying a comfortable life as a tenured professor at a prestigious university. But a personal crisis, an evangelical conversion, and a chance encounter in 1987 with Richard Dawkins's book *The Blind Watchmaker* when Johnson was on sabbatical leave in England thrust him into the creationism debate.

Johnson never pretended to be a scientist, and he recognized early on that the creation-scientists' claims of scientific legitimacy were flimsy at best and probably quixotic, so he sought to shift the grounds of debate from science to philosophy. In his influential 1991 book, *Darwin on Trial*, Johnson argued that scientists who preached evolution were not the impartial empiricists that they claimed to be. In fact, Johnson said, they brought their own presuppositions to their work, the presuppositions of materialism and naturalism. "Evolution, to them, means," he said, "a purposeless, material process propelled by random genetic changes." This bias, he continued, led scientists to preclude entirely the possibility that a creator lay behind the intricate wonders of creation. Evolutionary theory, Johnson charged, was the naturalists' "creation myth," which made it, in turn, a kind of religion. By the time of the centennial of the publication of *The Origin of Species*, Johnson wrote, "Darwinism was not just a theory of biology, but the most important element in a religion of scientific naturalism, with its own ethical agenda and plan for salvation through social and genetic engineering."[8]

Scientists, for the most part, remained impervious to Johnson's taunts. When I asked Leonard Kristhalka, a paleontologist then at the Carnegie Museum of Natural History in Pittsburgh, about Johnson's charge, he confessed immediately and unflinchingly. "I approach the study of science with naturalistic presuppositions," he said. "Scientists have nothing to say—certainly I as a scientist have nothing to say—about the existence or the nonexistence of God. That's not a scientific question."[9]

Johnson shrugged aside his critics, and he has since expanded his crusade to topple not only Darwin but also the two other materialist theorists whose work so shaped rational discourse in the twentieth century: Karl Marx and Sigmund Freud. Johnson's goal, in his words, is to construct "the case against naturalism" in science, law, and education.[10]

With Johnson having shifted the ground beneath the creationism debate, others rushed in to do the backing and filling, all the while giving credit to Johnson as their intellectual godfather. This movement became known as intelligent design, based on the notion that creation is so ordered and complex that some designer, an intelligent designer, must perforce have initiated and superintended the process. The intelligent-design theorists, following the lead of William Paley, a nineteenth-century clergyman, often cite the human eye as an example of the complexity of creation, which points to a creator.

Fair enough. Many people (including myself) would be inclined to agree with such a proposition and to accept on faith that a creator was in some way at work in bringing the world into being.

But faith alone has never been sufficient for the advocates of intelligent design. They want to "prove" their claims, to cloak their presuppositions with academic and scholarly legitimacy, and, thereby, to win legitimacy in scientific circles. But the stakes are even higher than they appear. If the Religious Right, in this case the proponents of intelligent design, can win acceptance for their ideas in the academy, then they will have breached the final barrier to their conquest of American society. Put another way, having captured all three branches of the federal government and having taken over the media (especially talk radio) and established a beachhead in Hollywood, the Republican–Religious Right coalition now seeks to consolidate its gains by winning acceptance in the academy, arguably the final line of defense against the juggernaut of conservativism.

Creationism, however, will not cut it in an academic context still dominated by Enlightenment rationalism. The Religious Right, then, had to find a way to compete with science to make the creationist case, and for that reason, the arguments of the biblical literalists have, well, evolved from Genesis to creationism to "scientific creationism" and now to intelligent design. But the larger strategy here goes beyond merely teaching creationism in school; it's far more nuanced, even insidious. The history of the creationist-evolution "debate" since the Scopes trial has been, in essence, the story of adaptation to new legal, social, and intellectual realities in order to win validation in educational circles.

To attain academic legitimacy, however, the Religious Right has chosen a peculiar strategy; they set about constructing a Trojan horse by cloaking creationism in the guise of science: intelligent design. But here is where the intelligent-design arguments dissolve into confusion and, at times, downright silliness. Intelligent-design advocates seek to substantiate their claims that a designer stands behind the creation process by all manner of argumentation, including mathematical probability calculations, or what one intelligent-design theorist calls "the logic of probabilistic inferences."[11]

Intelligent-design theorists are notoriously reticent about claiming publicly that God is responsible for creation, for that would give the movement's critics too obvious a reason to dismiss intelligent design as religion, not science. Instead, they purport to raise the *possibility* that an intelligent force was responsible for creation, though the ultimate goal of this strategy is an attack on science and the scientific method itself. "The question posed by intelligent design is not how we should do science and theology in light of the triumph of Enlightenment rationalism and scientific naturalism," one of the leading intelligent-design advocates wrote in 1999. "The question rather is how we should do science and theology in light of the impending collapse of Enlightenment rationalism and scientific naturalism."[12]

The first prong of attack for the advocates of intelligent design was to insinuate their ideas into the curricula of public schools. Rick Santorum, U.S. senator from Pennsylvania and a favorite of the Religious Right, inserted language into the 2001 "No Child Left Behind Act" urging educators to teach "the full range of scientific views that exist" on controversial topics "such as biological evolution." Conservatives in places as diverse as Dover, Pennsylvania, and Gull Lake, Michigan, have sought to force creationism and intelligent design into their science classrooms, or at least to sow doubts about evolution.[13]

In Dover, for instance, the school board required biology teachers to read a statement to the students asserting that Darwinism "is not a fact" and urging them "to keep an open mind." In the fall of 2005, the case went to trial. On December 20, 2005, U.S. District Judge John E. Jones, who had been appointed to the federal bench by George W. Bush, struck down the Dover requirement as an unconstitutional infringement of the separation of church and state. The judge's decision also addressed what he regarded as the central issue of the case: whether or not intelligent design was science. "The overwhelming evidence at trial established that ID is a religious view, a mere re-labeling of creationism, and not a scientific theory," Jones wrote. The judge criticized "the breathtaking inanity of the Board's decision" to pass intelligent design off as science. He added that "the argument of irreducible complexity, central to ID, employs the same flawed and illogical contrived dualism that doomed creation science in the 1980s."

The Dover decision dealt a temporary setback to the creationists, but it did not settle the matter. The issue of intelligent design has surfaced on a statewide level in Arkansas, Louisiana, Ohio, and Kansas; on August 2, 2005, George W. Bush opined to a group of Texas newspaper reporters that he thought intelligent design should be taught in public schools. A majority of Americans, according to polling data, agree.[14]

The intelligent-design movement benefits from a popular distrust of the scientific establishment, a suspicion that has been festering in American society for decades, even centuries. The push for science education in the 1960s led to all sorts of euphoric, almost messianic, talk about the benefits of science and technology. I remember well visiting the New York World's Fair as a nine-year-old in 1964. It was a wondrous display of all kinds of technological marvels, such as the whirring exhibitions of microwave ovens and futuristic modes of transportation. Five years later, we landed a man on the moon, and there seemed no limit to the possibilities of technological progress. Nuclear energy, scientists predicted, would make electricity so inexpensive that the power companies wouldn't bother to charge for it. Advances in science and technology were going to usher in a better world.

Already by the late 1960s, however, Americans had begun to have doubts. What Dwight Eisenhower had called the "military-industrial complex" was exterminating people with murderous efficiency in Vietnam, an increasingly unpopular war. The price of technology, it seemed, was environmental devastation, illustrated with unforgettable clarity when the Cuyahoga River caught fire on June 22, 1969, because of industrial contaminants in the water. The flames shot five stories into the sky. And what more spectacular demonstration of the failure of science and technology could there be than the *Challenger* disaster of January 29, 1986, the image of annihilation etched against the Florida sky?

Americans have been suspicious of science for decades now. It's no coincidence, in my judgment, that the resurgence of evangelicalism began in the early 1970s, abetted by the ignominy of Vietnam and the shame of Watergate, but also by the declining confidence in science. All that remains of the whirring technological exhibitions from the 1964–1965 World's Fair in Flushing, Queens, are rusting hulks. More important, Americans came to believe that while science and technology may have made our lives easier at some level—electric can openers and garage-door openers—science and technology haven't been able to teach us how to live, how to imbue our lives with meaning. Evangelicals generally, and the Religious Right in particular, have been able to exploit this vague sense of unease about the scientific establishment.

Taking their cue from the success of neoconservatives, creationists and the advocates of intelligent design have set up all manner of institutes and think tanks in an effort to lend legitimacy to their pursuits. Like the neoconservative groups that advocate supply-side economics or seek to ridicule or discredit the science behind global warming, these institutes tend to be interlocking and mutually reinforcing—the serpent devouring its own tail. These organizations, such as the Discovery Institute in Seattle, Washington, or the Intelligent Design Network, based in Shawnee Mission, Kansas, provide the illusion of "peer review" for their findings and thereby elude the scrutiny of the scientific community. In the course of the trial in Dover, Pennsylvania, Michael Behe, a biologist at Lehigh University and perhaps the most prominent academic to support intelligent design, conceded that "there are no peer reviewed articles by anyone advocating for intelligent design supported by pertinent experiments or calculations which provide detailed rigorous accounts of how intelligent design of any biological system occurred."[15]

The advocates for intelligent design, however, refuse to be diverted by their failure to publish in scientific journals recognized by the profession. Their tactic, rather, is to sow doubts about the credibility of evolution, in the same way that opponents of environmental protection insist that global warming has not been substantiated. "The important thing to remember is that like supply-side economics or global-warming skepticism, intelligent design doesn't have to attract significant support from actual researchers to be effective," Paul Krugman, a columnist for the *New York Times*, warned. "All it has to do is create confusion, to make it seem as if there really is a controversy about the validity of evolutionary theory." Indeed, intelligent design is most effective when it uses the language of science to establish its authority, all the while criticizing the philosophical underpinnings of science to inoculate the intelligent-design movement against critical evaluation of its pseudoscientific claims.[16]

The goal of these creationist and intelligent-design institutes is to attain academic respectability, though they seek to do so by circumventing the conventional mechanisms of peer review. While they very much want intelligent design taught in public schoolrooms, the biggest prize of all would be to win acceptance for intelligent design among the scientific community and among academics in major, nonsectarian universities.

On a pleasant spring evening on April 7, 2005, the intelligent-design advocates' road to legitimacy led through Dodds Auditorium in the venerable Woodrow Wilson School at Princeton University. A conservative organization, the Intercollegiate Studies Institute, based in Wilmington, Delaware, and the Arthur N. Rupe Foundation of Santa Barbara, California, set up a public debate, "Intelligent Design: Is It Science?" between Lee Silver, a professor of molecular biology at Princeton, and William A. Dembski, probably the foremost evangelist for intelligent design.[17]

The moderator introduced Silver as a graduate of the University of Pennsylvania in physics, a Ph.D. from Harvard in biophysics, and the author of nearly two hundred scholarly articles. Dembski himself is no slouch: bachelor's degree in psychology, master's degree in statistics, and doctorate in philosophy, all from the University of Illinois, Chicago; another doctorate in mathematics from the University of Chicago; and, finally, a Master of Divinity degree from Princeton Theological Seminary, the flagship Presbyterian seminary independent of, but geographically proximate to, Princeton University.

Wearing a dark suit slightly too large for his lanky frame, Dembski had the mien of an assistant vice president at a local bank or of someone who has just been dispatched to notify the next of kin. The moderator introduced him as having an unspecified affiliation with Baylor University, but that was somewhat misleading, and Dembski made no effort to correct the impression that he was a member of the faculty at Baylor.

Dembski's presence at Baylor, however, was nothing if not controversial. In 1999, Robert Sloan, then president of the university, approved the establishment of the Michael Polanyi Center under the aegis of the Baylor Institute for Faith and Learning and hired Dembski as director. Baylor's faculty, which was not consulted about either the center or about Dembski's appointment, was livid and voted overwhelmingly to ask the administration to dissolve the center, in part because the religion, science, and philosophy departments were not consulted. "I have never seen faculty as upset over any issue," Charles A. Weaver, associate professor of psychology and neuroscience, said. "It's just sheer outrage." Faculty in the sciences charged that Dembski was nothing more than a creationist who sought to embellish his views with pseudoscience. The Baylor administration agreed to convene an outside committee to review the center. The committee recommended that a faculty advisory panel oversee the science and religion components of the program and that the name of Michael Polanyi, a philosopher and chemist who died in 1976 and who had little interest in the notion of intelligent design, be dropped from the center's name.[18]

Sloan consented, acknowledging that he "should have handled more effectively the program's implementation." Dembski himself, however, was less than conciliatory, issuing a press release in which he gloated that the "dogmatic opponents of design who demanded the Center be shut down have met their Waterloo." Dembski, who never taught a single course at Baylor, was promptly relieved of his duties as director of the center, whereupon he accused the Baylor administration, which had supported him all along, of "intellectual McCarthyism." According to several sources, Dembski quietly completed his five-year contract as an untenured "associate research professor in the conceptual foundations of science" at some undisclosed location in central Texas, while concurrently holding the position of senior fellow with the Discovery Institute, a kind of omnibus Religious Right organization based in Seattle. Dembski also (in an uncanny demonstration of adaptability and natural selection) managed to snare an appointment as head of the Center for Science and Theology at Southern Baptist Theological Seminary in Louisville, Kentucky.

In his opening statement at the Princeton debate, Dembski talked about the complexity of species, which, he said, would be "hard to reproduce by chance." The human eye, he said, could not have been produced simply by evolution; it has "clear design characteristics." Scientists' "naturalistic, gradual explanations," he concluded, failed to account for the intricacy and variety of life. "I want to get you thinking," he told the audience, "that it *could* be" an intelligent force behind the created order.

Silver wondered why Dembski failed to mention God in his opening remarks, because that, in Silver's judgment, was what intelligent design was all about, the assertion that "God created the universe and continues to be involved." Silver argued against a single creative force behind each species, noting that chickens were bred from jungle fowl in northern India and that domestic dogs were descended from the Siberian wolf. "Human beings, not God, created dogs," he said. Other species evolved from what appeared to be random mistakes or mutations. Some alterations in the species came from "human-driven evolution," while others, like the development of dark pigmentation for people who live in the tropics as a protection against skin cancer, were the product of "natural evolution." The varieties found in the natural world, Silver said, could be explained as "a process of random mutation." That is the conclusion from science. "Intelligent design," he charged, "is based on faith, not science."

Dembski conceded that "we both agree that evolution has occurred" and that "natural selection certainly works," but Dembski insisted that scientific explanations were "limited in scope." When he resorted to the shopworn creationist criticism of "punctuated equilibrium," a theory developed by Niles Eldridge of the American Museum of Natural History and Stephen Jay Gould of

Harvard, Silver reclined in his chair and flashed a confident smile. Creationists for years have sought to discredit evolution by attacking punctuated equilibrium, the observation that the fossil record shows periods of intense geological activity and evolutionary change punctuated by eras of lesser activity. Duane Gish of the Institute for Creation Research routinely derides the Eldridge-Gould formulation as "herky-jerky," but Gould compared it to negotiating an incline by means of stair steps rather than climbing steadily up a ramp.

Though he had no trouble countering Dembski's arguments, Silver repeatedly expressed frustration at his opponent's evasiveness about intelligent design itself. At what point, for example, did the intelligent designer enter the creation process? Dembski wouldn't say, although he repeatedly offered vague platitudes like "Intelligence is a known causal power" and "We're asking the hard questions."

As a molecular biologist, Silver is no stranger to hard questions, but his empirical approach to knowledge contrasts sharply with that of a theologian or a philosopher. "Scientists don't pretend to know the truth," he said toward the end of the debate. "We keep an open mind if we are good scientists." He repeatedly challenged Dembski on the nature of his assertion that intelligent design was science and that it deserves to be taught as such. "Can you design an experiment that would describe an intelligent designer's handiwork?" Silver asked. Dembski did not respond. "The intelligent design claim is a claim from faith," Silver said. "Natural selection is a scientific hypothesis, and that's what I claim is the difference between the two." Silver returned, finally, to Dembski's evasiveness about the nature and the effect of intelligent design. "I've never learned how this thing is supposed to work," he said. "And for that reason, I don't think it's serious."

I confess that I've always been surprised by the passion that both sides—the scientists on the one hand and the creationists and intelligent-design advocates on the other—bring to the debate over origins. When PBS asked me to do a documentary on creationism in the mid-1990s, I developed a pattern of asking each person I interviewed what she or he thought was at stake in the creationist controversy. The responses astounded me. Clearly, many evangelicals felt that civilization itself hung in the balance.

Paul Lindstrom, head of Christian Liberty Academy in Arlington Heights, Illinois, said he thought of evolution as "rebellion against God." He added that the teaching of evolution in the schools conveyed the message that students were evolved from animals—and the students behaved accordingly, which, according to Lindstrom, led to all manner of deviant behavior among adolescents. "What I'm trying to do," Phillip Johnson of the University of California, Berkeley, said, "is to legitimate the critique of naturalism, the questioning of naturalism, in the universities. To put it the other way around, I'm trying to make it possible to ask theistic questions in the universities."[19]

Duane Gish of the Institute for Creation Research was the most expansive when asked why he had devoted his entire career to battling evolution. "Look what's happened in this country in the last fifty years," Gish began. He then offered a litany of social ills, ranging from "a rampant drug culture" to violence and crime. "Now I know a lot of evolutionists won't agree with me," he continued, "but I believe the major reason these things have happened is that our judges and our educators and our legislators, the leaders in our society, have been indoctrinated in evolutionary theory."[20]

Politicians associated with the Religious Right have also picked up on this argument. After the tragic shootings at Columbine High School in 1999, Tom DeLay, then majority leader of the House of Representatives, famously asserted that the cause of the rampage was that the students at Columbine were taught evolution.

When I put the what's-at-stake question to Dembski and Silver near the conclusion of their debate at Princeton, I received very different answers. Dembski muttered something evasive about wanting to allow for the possibility of an intelligent force, while Silver evoked images of schoolchildren in rural Mississippi forced to learn intelligent design in public school classrooms rather than study evolution, which Silver and other scientists regard as the foundation of science. Those children will be at a disadvantage, he said, and the replication of that pattern elsewhere "is not going to lead to a productive country."

Silver's assessment of what's at stake is accurate, but he underestimates the even larger agenda at work here. In effect, the creationist/intelligent-design movement aspires to replace science, or physics, with metaphysics. The assertion of theistic origins and the substitution of religiously grounded assertions for the empirically based pursuit of scientific knowledge may satisfy some evangelicals and more than a few Roman Catholics, but it is unlikely to advance scientific inquiry.

The attempt to "baptize" creationism or intelligent design as science, moreover, demeans both religion and science by confusing the categories. Paradoxically, when the Religious Right asserts that intelligent design is science, it implies that faith in God or in the reliability of the scriptures is inadequate, that it needs the imprimatur of the scientific method. This subjects religious belief to the canons of Enlightenment rationalism because it concedes, at least by inference, that faith is not sufficient in itself. On the other side of the equation, the intelligent-design movement demands that scientists answer questions—about the existence of God or an intelligent designer—that the scientific method is incapable of asking.

For the Religious Right, however, intelligent design is the camel's nose under the tent flap. If Dembski and his colleagues succeed in insinuating intelligent design into the curriculum of public schools, they will have won a crucial victory in their crusade to breach the wall of separation between church and state. Through the teaching of creationism in the schools, no less than through school vouchers or tax-supported religious schools, the Religious Right wants the state to propagate religious beliefs—more particularly, the beliefs of one religious tradition to the exclusion of all others.

Beyond public schools, however, the even larger prize for the advocates of intelligent design is higher education, because the Religious Right realizes that, as with all major movements in American history from the colonial era to the present, the way to change society is to reform education. Colleges and universities have been important throughout American history as the engines of culture as manifested in music, art, and ideas. If generations of college students can be convinced of the scientific merits of intelligent design, then they will transmit those ideas to the remainder of society in their roles as parents and, especially, as teachers.

The real quest behind the intelligent-design movement, then, is academic respectability, which is why debates like the one at Princeton are strategically important to the Religious Right. Despite all of the Right's bluster about the so-called liberal media—What liberal media? Try spinning the radio dial—the last line of defense against the Right, after the corporatization of media interests, the somnolence of mainline Protestantism, and the wheezing of the Democratic Party, is the academy.

Intelligent-design advocates have managed to place a few of their own in academic positions—Michael Behe, the biologist at Lehigh University, is probably the most prominent—but they haven't yet been able to penetrate the scholarly community in a large-scale way. This is not for lack of trying. The Discovery Institute claims to have recruited more than five hundred scientists to sign a document that reads, "We are skeptical of claims for the ability of random mutation and natural selection to account for the complexity of life. Careful examination of the evidence for Darwinian theory should be encouraged."

If intelligent design wins scholarly credibility or even scientific credibility, if Phillip Johnson's aspiration to "make it possible to ask theistic questions in the universities" comes to pass, then even larger, more profound changes will be possible: America's institutions of higher education could once again serve to propagate the faith, in which case, they will have come full circle because many of the nation's colleges and universities were founded for the education and training of clergy. The Puritans of New England formed Harvard in 1636, "dreading to leave an illiterate Ministry to the Churches, when our present Ministers shall lie in the Dust." Yale College was formed in 1701, a reaction in part to the perceived liberalism at Harvard. The College of New Jersey (now Princeton) evolved out of the Log College, a home-based seminary for the training of Presbyterian clergy. Dartmouth began as Moor's Charity School for the preparation of Indians for missionary work, and the great wave of college formation in the nineteenth century represented an attempt on the part of Protestant denominations, Methodists and Presbyterians especially, to evangelize and to civilize the West.[21]

Farfetched as it sounds, the Religious Right would love nothing more than to secure these institutions of higher learning for confessional purposes. And who could blame them?

The campaign to reclaim these universities received a boost from George M. Marsden, the Francis A. McAnaney Professor of History at the University of Notre Dame. In 1994, Marsden published *The Soul of the American University*, an influential jeremiad about the absence of faith in the academy. In the book and in several related forums, Marsden asserted, with scant corroborating evidence, that "many academics seem uncritically to hold that religiously-based viewpoints are by definition no better than second class," that people with religious convictions today are unwelcome in the academy, and that "the free exercise of religion does not extend to the dominant intellectual centers of our culture."[22]

The Soul of the American University was William F. Buckley's *God and Man at Yale* on steroids in that Marsden expanded his indictment of higher education beyond New Haven to encompass virtually every American university, especially those that had been founded by Protestants for Protestants. Yale was no longer a safe haven for Congregationalists, he lamented, or Princeton for Presbyterians. Indeed, Marsden demonstrated that many of America's institutions of higher learning were no longer "nurseries of piety," that they no longer devoted themselves exclusively to the training of evangelical ministers. All well and good, though it was hardly the breaking news that it might have been several centuries earlier.

This was music to the ears of the Religious Right, eager to portray universities as hostile to faith and thereby to discredit—even to demolish—the last line of resistance to their agenda. A large number of scholars who call themselves evangelicals have in fact found acceptance at major "secular" universities; many would be considered at or near the pinnacle of their fields. But these evangelicals did not attain their lofty positions in prestigious universities because of special pleading; they got there because of their scholarship, because they played by the rules of academic discourse, and because (unlike the advocates of intelligent design) they excelled by submitting their work to the critical analysis of their respective guilds. Although I would not be so naïve as to suggest that the university is a perfect meritocracy—I have my own quiver of anecdotes on that point—evangelicals in the academy did not reach the top of the ivory tower by catapult or by camouflaging their religious convictions as science. They ascended step by step, more or less like everybody else.

The Religious Right persistently dismisses colleges and universities as bastions of liberalism. To the extent that many professors tilt toward the political left, that is probably true, making the academy perhaps the final barrier against the tide of conservativism at the turn of the twenty-first century. In another sense, however, the academy is profoundly *conservative* in that it subjects the work of its members to repeated and merciless scrutiny—in peer review for scholarly publication and in the tenure and promotion process. The scholarship that fails to pass muster is discarded, while that which is compelling and persuasive eventually, slowly, wins acceptance.

Despite the bluster of its advocates, intelligent design has failed to meet the standards for scientific credibility. As Behe conceded in the Dover, Pennsylvania, trial, the proponents of intelligent design even refuse to submit their "scholarship" to peer-reviewed scientific journals because they know it will be rejected for failing to adhere to the rules of scientific inquiry. They, along with George Marsden, can claim antireligious bias in the academy, but their histrionics are misplaced. Intelligent design is religion, not science, and the proper venue for the propagation of faith is the home or the church, not the university.

As an evangelical Christian, moreover, I'm afraid that I don't share Marsden's apparent confidence in institutions, academic or otherwise, as guarantors of faith and piety. In fact, history (as I read it) suggests that institutions are remarkably poor vessels for the perpetuation of faith, and if Marsden believes that the cause of the gospel will be markedly advanced by remaking American universities into redoubts of piety or confessionalism, I think his confidence is utterly misplaced. What, after all, was the Protestant Reformation all about?[23]

The Dembski-Silver debate at Princeton, then, should be viewed in the context of a larger attempt to win academic respectability, to reclaim institutions of higher education for confessional ends, and, in so doing, to advance the agenda of the Religious Right. A school like Princeton is, in a sense, the ultimate prize, both because of its prestige in the intellectual world and because of its eighteenth-century history as an institution for the education of clergy. For

Dembski, the content or the outcome of the debate was less important than the debate itself because his very presence in a university forum lent credence to his ideas.

Indeed, each party in the debate over origins speaks a different language: scientists the language of empirical knowledge derived from the application of the scientific method through experiment and careful, painstaking examination of the fossil record, and creationists the language of faith as derived from the scriptures. One asserts that God initiated the process of creation, and the other seeks to explain how earlier forms of life developed into their current iterations. Those different languages have different criteria for ascertaining truth, just as a mathematician and an art historian have different ways of solving problems peculiar to their fields and arriving at conclusions that their colleagues will find persuasive. As a believer, I have no problem accepting that God, in some way that I cannot fully explain, is responsible for the created order, but that is an assertion of faith, not a conclusion vindicated by scientific inquiry, for I know of no experiment to test empirically for the presence of God.

"The problem with intelligent-design theory is not that it is false but that it is not falsifiable," George F. Will, a conservative, wrote in his *Newsweek* column on the occasion of the eightieth anniversary of the Scopes trial. "Not being susceptible to contradicting evidence, it is not a testable hypothesis. Hence it is not scientific but a creedal test—a matter of faith, unsuited to a public school's science curriculum." Intelligent design purports to answer a question—Who is responsible for the created order?—that scientists would not dare to ask because they have no way outside the claims of faith and within the canons of the scientific method to pose the question, much less formulate an answer. "I have no idea where the first molecule came from," Lee Silver conceded at the conclusion of the debate in Princeton, but that does not deter him from trying to chart and to ascertain the development of various life forms.[24]

William Dembski and the intelligent-design advocates have every right to claim that God is responsible for the created order. I happen to agree with them. But their warrant for making such a claim lies within the canon of scripture, not the canons of science. I have no objections to intelligent design being taught in theological seminaries or religious studies curricula or even philosophy class-rooms, though I think the more appropriate venue is Sunday school—and I don't mean that facetiously because the proper arena for the propagation of the faith is the church or synagogue or mosque or temple or, even better, the home. Until Dembski and his colleagues can devise experiments consistent with the scientific method to test their claims, they should stop parading as scientists.

Dembski and the intelligent-design folks may or may not be good philosophers and theologians; I'm not qualified to judge. As scientists, however, if the debate at Princeton was any indication, they still have a long way to go to attain the intellectual legitimacy they so desperately crave.

The debate over intelligent design is crucial because, given the importance of education in shaping American society, this is a bat-tle for the future. For conservatives and for the Religious Right, intelligent design is something akin to a battering ram; they want to use it to breach the fortress of the academy, arguably the final line of defense against conservativism. If they can win intellectual legiti-macy for their views, then their conquest of American society will be complete.

Is this a proper function for the faith? If George Marsden and William Dembski have their way, the academy will become a locus for the propagation not only of piety, but of a particular, narrow piety that, in the present context at least, carries with it considerable political baggage. It's understandable that Marsden would want to lament the fact that America's major universities no longer perform a catechetical function. But American Protestants, evangelicals in particular, have devised other institutions—church-related colleges, seminaries, and Sunday schools—to carry out that task.

America's evangelicals should take considerable pride in the fact that they have bequeathed to American society such distinguished universities as Princeton, which originated during the Great Awakening of the 1740s. No, Princeton no longer retains the confessional moorings that constrained it in 1746, when the school first opened its doors, a circumstance that merely underscores the point that institutions are woefully inadequate as guarantors of faith.

But Princeton and places like it guarantee the perpetuation of other important values in American life, not least of which is the intellectual freedom to pursue ideas untrammeled by confessional agendas. Dembski and his intelligent-design brethren can bemoan the fact that their ideas have not won acceptance in the public schools or in the academy, but that is due not to bias (as they contend) but to the fact that they have yet to persuade anyone in the courts or the scientific community that intelligent design is anything other than religion.

Until Dembski and his colleagues can convince the academic community that they are doing real science, intelligent design will remain, in the words of one observer during the Dover trial, nothing more than creationism in a cheap tuxedo. Dembski apparently fails to recognize that faith—in this case, faith in the existence of an intelligent designer—has its own integrity and that to seek the validation of religious belief as science demeans the faith by allowing the canons of Enlightenment rationalism to serve as the final arbiter of truth.

George Marsden's vision is equally misguided, not to say quixotic. America's universities play a vital role in American life as places where, as in public schools, we confront the challenges of living in a pluralistic context. Contrary to Marsden's assertions, people of faith are welcome in that environment, but they have to compete on an equal footing in the marketplace of ideas, unlike Dembski and his colleagues, who refuse to engage in that competition. The example of Princeton, however, instructs us in the dangers of tying faith to institutions. Religious belief flourishes best outside of institutional constraints and without the imprimatur of schools, the state, and the university.

chapter 5

Voices in the Wilderness

Evangelicals and the Environment

*Oh, God, enlarge within us the sense of fellowship with
all living things, our brothers the animals to whom
Thou gavest the earth in common with us. We
remember with shame that in the past we have
exercised the high dominion of man with ruthless
cruelty so that the voice of the earth, which should have
gone up to thee in song, has been a groan of travail.*
—Saint Basil, bishop of Caesarea, ca. 375

It requires no great leap of logic to surmise that evangelicals, most of whom insist that a creator or an intelligent designer superintended the creation process, would want to situate themselves in the front ranks of the environmental movement. If you believe that God is responsible for the created order, and especially if you believe so fervently that you want intelligent design taught as science, then surely you will have a vested interest in conservation and caring for the wonders of creation.

Sadly, that has not always been the case. In its early years, the Religious Right, following the conservative and business-friendly orthodoxy of the Reagan administration, neglected environmental matters altogether. More recently, leaders of the Religious Right have joined neoconservatives in seeking to drill for oil in the Arctic National Wildlife Refuge, to weaken the provisions of the Endangered Species Act, or to debunk global warming.

Yet, at the same time that the leaders of the Religious Right have been marching in lockstep with the Republican Party, a growing number of rank-and-file evangelicals have begun to question, and even to challenge, the antienvironmentalism of the Religious Right. This insurgency by evangelicals with an environmental conscience has the potential to disrupt the alliance between evangelicals and the Republican Party. Many evangelicals are beginning to recognize, almost intuitively, that the wanton abuse of natural resources is fundamentally incompatible with a view of creation as God's handiwork. The fissure between evangelicals and the leaders of the Religious Right is small, but it is large enough to admit a ray of light, and it represents a considerable change in attitude from the early years of the Religious Right.

In January 1988, when I was tracking evangelicals on the snowy campaign trail of the Iowa precinct caucuses and the New Hampshire primary, several Religious Right activists were all atwitter about a book by Constance Cumbey, an evangelical who described herself as "the noted attorney from Detroit, Michigan." This book, *Hidden Dangers of the Rainbow: The New Age Movement and Our Coming Age of Barbarism*, purported to disclose the nefarious forces behind everything from hunger relief to the environmental movement. The ranks of those who expressed concern for the ecological health of the world, Cumbey asserted, were filled with neopagans and New Agers. She excoriated such organizations as the

Sierra Club and warned that the New Age movement was infiltrating American society through all manner of devious schemes, including "Whole Earth catalogs, many health food stores and vegetarian restaurants, disarmament campaigns, and nearly every other social cause, including animal liberation!"[1]

I'm not persuaded that Cumbey's book changed the minds of many evangelicals in the late 1980s. More likely, especially during an earlier era of fierce partisanship, it gave political conservatives the excuse they needed to shy away from an issue more commonly associated with the Democratic Party. For decades, evangelicals have neglected the environment because it seemed to them unimportant in their grander scheme of biblical interpretation. Cumbey herself signaled this approach when she wrote, "Jesus clearly warned that conditions would grow worse and worse until His return."[2]

Evangelical views of the environment, and their attitudes toward society itself, have a long and complicated history, one that has been tied inextricably to their understanding of biblical prophecies. Evangelicals in the antebellum period believed that the construction of a millennial kingdom, the thousand years of righteousness described in Revelation 20, would precede the Second Coming of Jesus. This mode of biblical interpretation, known as *postmillennialism* because it held that Jesus would return to earth after the millennium, provided a powerful impetus for the improvement of society. Postmillennialists believed that they, as the followers of Jesus, could bring on the millennium now—right here on earth and, more specifically, right here in America—by dint of their own efforts.

Postmillennialism animated many of the social-reform movements of the mid-nineteenth century: abolitionism, temperance, prison reform, women's rights, and the like. Lyman Beecher, for instance, mounted a campaign against dueling after Aaron Burr, then vice president of the United States, killed Alexander Hamilton in Weehawken, New Jersey, in 1804. Beecher initiated such a campaign because he believed that dueling was not a feature appropriate to the millennial age. The evangelical conviction that Jesus would return to earth after the millennium, then, served as a powerful incentive for social amelioration. Evangelicals believed that they were responsible for constructing the heavenly city of Zion here on earth.[3]

As the nineteenth century wore on, however, the carnage of the Civil War began to trigger doubts about postmillennialism, and by the closing decades of the nineteenth century, evangelicals looked around and saw the effects of urbanization, industrialization, and the influx of non-Protestant immigrants (who didn't share evangelical scruples about temperance). The teeming tenements of the Lower East Side of Manhattan, beset by labor unrest, hardly resembled the postmillennial kingdom that evangelicals had confidently predicted earlier in the century, so they searched for a new mode of biblical interpretation that better fit the temper of the times.

John Nelson Darby, a member of the Plymouth Brethren Church in England, provided a theological argument to explain this state of affairs. Evangelical expectations that Jesus would return after they had constructed a millennial kingdom were all wrong, Darby insisted. He provided an alternative interpretation of the apocalyptic passages in the scriptures that he called *dispen-*

sationalism or *dispensational premillennialism*. According to this theory, all of human history could be divided into different ages or dispensations, and it asserted that God had dealt differently with humanity in each of these dispensations. The Almighty had struck a particular deal with Noah and with Abraham, for instance, and with the ancient Israelites, his "chosen people." But the most important tenet of dispensational thought was that Jesus could return to earth at any moment *before* the millennium (thus the term *premillennialism*).

Dispensationalism spread quickly among theologically conservative Protestants during the decades surrounding the turn of the twentieth century, and the ramifications of this theological shift were enormous. Evangelicals used premillennialism as an excuse to withdraw from campaigns of social reform, for example, in order to devote their full attention to preparations for the Second Coming of Jesus, which entailed cultivating inner piety and trying to convert others to the faith. In the face of mounting social ills, evangelicals shifted their attentions from the long term to the short term—because the time was so brief, they believed, until the return of Jesus. "I look upon this world as a wrecked vessel," the Chicago evangelist Dwight L. Moody declared. "God has given me a lifeboat and said, 'Moody, save all you can.'"

The wholesale adoption of dispensational premillennialism, then, had several ramifications. First, evangelicals largely abandoned efforts to reform society and focused their energies on individual regeneration. Second, now fixated on the world to come, evangelicals were freed from worries about the maintenance of this world, which they came to regard as fallen and transitory.

The effects of dispensational thought marked evangelicalism throughout most of the twentieth century. The belief in dispensational premillennialism, for instance, helps to explain why evangelicals have produced such bad architecture, why functionalism almost invariably trumps art. Why invest your resources in buildings or ornamentation when Jesus will return at any time? But it has also informed their attitudes toward the environment, attitudes that, until recently, have ranged from benign neglect to outright exploitation. The rationale went something like this: Since Jesus is coming back to earth at any moment, why concern yourself with water quality or with the ozone layer when the apocalyptic return of Jesus to usher in a new world will render any such worries irrelevant?

No one person illustrated the ruinous policy effects of dispensationalism better than James G. Watt, a member of the Assemblies of God denomination and Ronald Reagan's first secretary of the interior, the agency ostensibly responsible for the protection of the environment. Watt, in fact, took dispensationalism even further, from a neglect of the natural world to outright exploitation. "We will mine more, drill more, cut more timber," he promised. Watt starkly expressed his theological rationale before Congress during his confirmation hearings. On February 5, 1981, less than three weeks into the Reagan presidency, Watt suggested that he was not overly concerned about preserving the environment because the imminent Second Coming of Jesus ultimately would render all such efforts irrelevant. "I don't know how many future generations we can count on before the Lord returns," he said, adding, "whatever it is we have to manage with a skill to leave the resources needed for future generations."[4]

For Watt, however, "management" meant development and exploitation. As secretary of the interior, he cut funding for the protection of endangered species and sold oil and gas leases in wilderness areas. He sought to eliminate the Land and Water Conservation Fund and cut substantially the government's regulations protecting the environment.

Watt, described by the Audubon Society as "arguably the most antienvironment secretary ever," reflected the antienvironmental sensibilities of his boss, who famously remarked that if you'd seen one redwood tree, you'd seen them all. But another ideology popular with evangelicals has also contributed to the exploitation of the environment on their part. The notion of "dominion," propagated by E. Calvin Beisner, formerly of Covenant College (Tennessee) and now associated with Knox Theological Seminary in Fort Lauderdale, Florida, asserts that God has placed all of nature at the disposal of humanity. The created order has no intrinsic value aside from how it benefits human beings. Beisner argues, for example, that God has ceded control of, or "dominion" over, creation to humanity and that our sole concern as God's agents is "the management of the resources God has providentially put at our disposal." Standing at the pinnacle of creation, then, humanity is free to use the natural world, "lifting it out of unfruitful bondage and into productive liberty." There is no higher entity than humanity itself, according to Beisner. "All of our acquisitive activities should be undertaken with the purpose of extending godly rule, or dominion."[5]

Beisner's dominion theology, the notion that humanity stands at the apex of creation, has affinities with the "wise use" movement, which emerged in the early 1980s—coincident with Watt's tenure as secretary of the interior and with the emergence of the Religious

Right. Proponents argue that the wise use of land and natural resources overrides environmental considerations. Like other antienvironmental groups, the wise use movement places humanity
above the rest of the created order, which authorizes, for instance,
the unfettered extraction of minerals by mining corporations, the
clear-cutting of forests by logging interests, and unlimited access to
public lands by hunters and off-road vehicle owners.

Dominion theology and wise use ideology also inform humanity's relationship with other creatures. Trophy hunters or the corporate owners of factory farms, where hogs or chickens see nary a
ray of sunshine for their entire miserable lives, need not fret over
the suffering they inflict on animals because God has given humanity dominion over animals. Dominion theologians refer to the "dominion" account in Genesis 1, the passage routinely used by
antienvironmentalists to justify human exploitation of the rest of
the created order. "And God said, Let us make man in our image,
after our likeness," the passage reads, "and let them have dominion
over the fish of the sea, and over the foul of the air, and over the cattle, and over all the earth, and over every creeping thing that creep-
eth upon the earth." For those who want to exploit the created
order, this verse provides the only justification they need.[6]

That narrow interpretation, however, ignores an earlier passage, which reads, "And God created whales, and every living
creature that moveth, which the waters brought forth abundantly,
after their kind, and every winged foul after his kind: and God saw
that it was good." Elsewhere in the Hebrew Bible, the Psalmist
writes, "The Lord is good to all: and his tender mercies are over
all his works." Seen in this larger context, "dominion" positions
humanity less in terms of power and exploitation than as servant

and advocate for all of creation. This broader reading makes it difficult to reconcile "tender mercies" with environmental desecration or with the hunting of confined animals for sport or with strip-mining or with the squeals of a not-yet-dead animal hanging from a slaughterhouse hook.[7]

This more contextual reading of Genesis 1 casts serious doubts on dominion theology. It also discredits the canard that Religious Right activists employ most often to dismiss environmental concerns: a diminished or inadequate anthropology (doctrine of humanity). Once they have exhausted the tired neopagan and New Age accusations, opponents of environmentalism typically trot out the argument that treating God's creation with respect somehow compromises the theological precept that humanity stands at the pinnacle of creation. Charles Colson, for instance, one of the intellectual leaders of the Religious Right, wrote that "animal-rights proponents are serious—and dangerous" because they compromise on the issue of anthropocentrism. Wesley J. Smith, a senior fellow at the Discovery Institute, the Religious Right think tank in Seattle, dismisses the suffering and the death of animals during experimentation as a "regrettable necessity" and accuses animal-rights activists of a "dark misanthropy."[8]

The currency of dominion theology and wise use ideology among leaders of the Religious Right also helps to explain their fixation on abortion and their relative lack of interest in environmental matters. If humanity stands at the head of creation, then all else fades into irrelevance. Evangelicals' fixation on the abortion issue in recent years has so reified the notion of humanity as the apex of the created order that evangelicals have neglected entirely other elements of God's creation. For evangelicals, who hold ostensibly to the doctrine of human depravity (the belief that humanity in its natural state is fallen), this is a curious argument. Anthropocentrism elevates humanity above the remainder of creation, which then confers a license to exploit natural resources at will. This is especially pernicious when combined with a dispensationalist reading of the Bible (as with James Watt), which views the natural world purely in functional terms: How can the natural world, including animals, benefit *me*—feed me, clothe me, enrich me?

This anthropocentrism is abundantly evident in the agenda of the Religious Right. Many of the same people who routinely excoriate pro-choice advocates and who portray themselves as champions of the "preborn" have precious little to say about the destruction of the environment, the cruelty of factory farms, the consumer mentality, and the quest for material comforts. How many Americans, evangelicals included, engage in recreational shopping, for instance, oblivious to the environmental impact of their actions or their marketplace decisions? Even more to the point, how can anyone miss the irony that the ranks of those opposed to abortion, who profess to hear a "fetal scream," are remarkably deaf to squeals of live animals hanging from meat hooks in the abattoir?

The combination of dominion theology from the Religious Right and the wise use ideology of corporate and business interests has created a powerful coalition to oppose environmental protections. All of the antienvironmental groups associated with the Religious Right appear to be connected with one another and with corporate interests in an intricate spiderweb. Calvin Beisner, the dominion theologian, for instance, is an adjunct scholar of the Acton Institute for the Study of Religion and Liberty, a pro-business group based in Grand Rapids, Michigan, that sits at the intersection of neoconservativism and the Religious Right. The Acton Institute, formed in 1990, takes money from corporations like ExxonMobil and from such right-wing groups as the Scaife Family Foundation, the John M. Olin Foundation, and the DeVos family of Amway fame. On environmental matters, the organization's website states, "Acton Institute recognizes that a strong, vibrant economy and a vigorous commitment to property rights are essential to creating the necessary incentives for sound ecological stewardship practices."

Beisner is also a member of the advisory committee of the Interfaith Council for Environmental Stewardship and a member of the "board of academic and scientific advisors" for the Committee for a Constructive Tomorrow, yet another pro-business group. Robert Sirico, head of the Acton Institute, is also on the board for the Committee for a Constructive Tomorrow and on the advisory committee of the Interfaith Council for Environmental Stewardship.

And so it goes—a complex network of individuals and organizations. But it is a web of deception and subterfuge. Funded lavishly by corporate interests and hard-right conservatives, these organizations seek not to protect the environment but rather to free corporations from environmental regulations, to attack such landmark legislation as the Endangered Species Act, and to debunk global warming due to atmospheric pollution, which has produced dramatic changes in weather patterns over the past several decades.[9]

In October 1999, twenty-five Religious Right leaders met in West Cornwall, Connecticut, to devise strategies for countering the environmental movement. The group accused religious leaders inclining toward environment protection of naïveté, charging that "their passion is often based on a romantic view of nature, a misguided distrust of science and technology, and an intense focus on problems that are highly speculative and largely irrelevant to meeting our obligations to the world's poor." The group, which echoes the pro-business and antiregulatory sentiments of political conservatives, produced the Cornwall Declaration on Environmental Stewardship and formed the equally deceptively named Interfaith Council for Environmental Stewardship, a coalition of Religious Right leaders aiming to counteract the environmental movement.

Among the most insidious tactics employed by neoconservatives and antienvironmental groups in recent years are euphemism and outright deception. The Bush administration's actions to repeal provisions of the "Clean Air Act" and thereby allow corporations greater freedom to pollute, for example, was called the "Clear Skies" program; the "Healthy Forests" initiative encourages destructive logging of old-growth forests.

The antienvironmentalist leaders of the Religious Right have followed suit. The Cornwall Declaration on Environmental Stewardship is a masterpiece of this kind of deception, issuing as it did, ironically, from the bucolic hills of northwestern Connecticut. The declaration, in fact, is a brief for industry and corporate interests. It opens with a pious affirmation of "shared reverence for God and His creation and love for our neighbors" and professes that the signatories are "committed to justice and compassion." Reverence, however, has its limits. "A clean environment is a costly good," the declaration warns; "consequently, growing affluence, technological innovation, and the application of human and material capital are integral to environmental improvement." The statement dismisses as "unfounded" all the "fears of destructive manmade global warming, overpopulation, and rampant species loss." The Cornwall Declaration concludes with a statement of faith in "advancements in agriculture, industry, and commerce" and looks to a future of unbridled capitalism, "a world in which widespread economic freedom—which is integral to private, market economies—makes sound ecological stewardship available to ever greater numbers."

The list of signatories to the Cornwall Declaration reads like a who's who of the Religious Right, including, among others, James Dobson of Focus on the Family; Charles Colson of Prison Fellowship; Michael Cromartie, vice president of the Ethics and Public Policy Center; Donald Wildmon, head of the American Family Association; and D. James Kennedy, pastor of Coral Ridge Presbyterian Church and president of Knox Theological Seminary. With the production of a statement like that, I'm confident that ExxonMobil and Dickie Scaife were well satisfied with what their money had purchased.

A growing number of evangelicals, however, refuse to be bullied into accepting an ideology that they believe intuitively is wrong. The Cornwall Declaration may have attracted the predictable Greek chorus of Religious Right leaders, but other evangelicals are beginning to dissent from the hard-right orthodoxy of the Religious Right, especially on matters relating to the environment.

On a chilly afternoon in late December, beneath a steely gray sky, a couple of dozen college students from a variety of evangelical schools trundled through the snows of northern Michigan. "Just a subtle difference in elevation can make a major difference in the natural community," David Mahan called out to the group as they looked down on a small kettle lake, carved by glaciers thousands of years ago. He informed the students that he had seen ospreys and bald eagles in the area and that the woods here consisted primarily of black spruce and balsam fir. Then, pointing to the surrounding forest, Mahan noted the effects of deer on the woodlands. "We have more deer than the habitat can support in northern vegetation," he said.

Farther along, Chris Newhouse, a professor of biology at Spring Arbor University, pointed out the presence of snow fleas, the tiny black dots atop the snow that I had always assumed were inanimate. He noted the work of a pileated woodpecker on a nearby tree, and as the hike bent around the edges of a beaver pond, Newhouse talked at length about the habitat for grouse and snowshoe hares. A large black animal skittered across the snow in the distance. Robert Barr, who has lived in the area for the better part of three decades, asked the students to notice the different stands of woods all around them. The contrast is striking all throughout the region of northern Michigan in the area around Traverse City; one patch of trees is softwoods or conifers, while the adjacent acreage consists entirely of hardwoods. Barr explained that the woodlands of the area alternate between Great Lakes pine forest and northern hardwoods. Birches and aspens, he noted, don't reproduce in their own shade.

Here in Blue Lake Township, near the town of Mancelona, natural history has been tied inextricably to human history, at least over the past century or two. Barr told the students that the region had a larger human population in 1900 than it does today; however, poor management of the environment brought on natural and economic calamity from which the area has not fully recovered. From 1917 to

1919, Barr said, logging interests clear-cut the pine forests of the
area. Then, they clear-cut the stands of hardwoods. Finally, with
the land denuded of trees, a huge fire swept through in 1923, con-
suming the detritus of the remaining brush and debris. The local
economy was devastated, and 85 percent of the township's land re-
verted to state ownership for nonpayment of taxes. Only now, decades later, does the natural world show signs of recovery. The
local economy, however, lags behind.

The Au Sable Institute for Environmental Studies sits on a sixty-
five-acre site in Blue Lake Township adjacent to Louie's Pond,
across the road from Big Twin Lake and part of the Manistee River
watershed. The institute evolved out of evangelical concerns for the
well-being of the natural world, and it seeks "the integration of
knowledge of the Creation with biblical principles for the purpose
of bringing the Christian community and the general public to a
better understanding of the Creator and the stewardship of God's
Creation." Toward that end, according to promotional materials,
"its programs and activities are structured to allow, and are conducted for, promotion of Christian environmental stewardship."

The notion of "stewardship" is important to David Mahan, associate director of the Au Sable Institute. Just prior to the hike, he
gave a lecture entitled "Practicing a Sense of Place: A Northern
Michigan Example." Mahan, who holds a Ph.D. in aquatic ecology
from Michigan State University, opened with a question: "What's
our role on the earth as Christians?" Believers, he said, were called
to be stewards of creation, and he marshaled a series of biblical
texts to substantiate his arguments. "God values all that he has
made," Mahan said, "and we should too." He cited the examples of
the Spotted Owl, Kirtland's Warbler, and Dwarf Lake Iris—all of

them endangered species and the latter two native to Michigan. The responsibility of stewardship, Mahan said, entails first an understanding of creation and then a duty to restore and protect it. "What we do in this life really matters," he said.

The students seated before him took careful notes. In addition to providing environmental education programs for children in kindergarten through twelfth grade, Au Sable offers courses on the environment here at its Great Lakes campus in northern Michigan during the summer and in late December through early January, between semesters. The institute also has satellite programs in southern Florida, India, and Africa and a Pacific Rim campus on Whidbey Island in Puget Sound. College students, all of them from evangelical schools, participate in the Au Sable programs and earn academic credit from their colleges, schools like North Park University (Illinois), Messiah College (Pennsylvania), Cornerstone University (Michigan), Bethel University (Minnesota), Spring Arbor University (Michigan), Anderson University (Indiana), and Calvin College (Michigan).

Each winter at Au Sable, Rolf Bouma, chaplain for the Christian Reformed Church at the University of Michigan, teaches a seminar called "Environmental Ethics," an offering grounded more in the humanities than in science. He noted that environmental ethics, which he defines as "a discourse that attempts to understand human relationships with and toward the non-human world," is a relatively new discipline, one that has emerged only in the last thirty years or so, roughly coincident with the environmental movement. Bouma added that environmental ethics challenges the entire foundation of traditional ethical discourse. Whereas traditional ethics ascribes worth or "moral considerability" only to human beings, environmental ethics rejects those anthropocentric assumptions and insists that human beings have a responsibility to entities beyond humanity. In staking out such a position, Bouma and other evangelicals like him seek to counter the arguments of dominion theology and wise use ideology that have been used to quash environmental consciousness.[10]

Some of the students attend the Au Sable Institute simply to fulfill a science requirement or to shore up their transcripts. Others, like Peter Carlson of North Park University, were attracted precisely because of the curriculum. "I really like plants and ecology," he told me during another of Au Sable's hikes through the area. "And I got even more impassioned about it here." Wendy Klooster is one of many students who are so impressed with the people and the courses that they look for ways to maintain a connection with Au Sable. Klooster, a recent graduate of Anderson University, credits the Au Sable programs in Michigan and on Whidbey Island with being a "major influence" on her decision to study botany and horticulture. She works in a maintenance position now at the Michigan campus but hopes to begin graduate school soon; in ten years, she wants to be married, settled somewhere, and working in horticulture.

A few of the students at Au Sable happily described themselves as "tree-huggers," while others like Thomas Dean of Greenville, Michigan, a student at Cornerstone University who spends his summers working on a farm, weren't so sure. "I think there needs to be a balance between modern practices and the kind of sustainable agriculture they talk about here," he said. When I asked Rachel Wolf, a student at Calvin College who grew up in Princeton, Illinois, whether she considered herself an environmentalist,

she responded tentatively. "Yeah, I guess," she said, her eyes shifting nervously, "but I wouldn't blow something up," an apparent
reference to those she considered environmental extremists.

This kind of furtive reaction betrays the uneasiness that some
evangelicals have about challenging the hard-right orthodoxy of
the Religious Right. Among evangelicals, owing in part to the mischief wrought by Constance Cumbey and others, there's still some
residual suspicion of environmentalism as a form of neopaganism
or New Age devotion, and some colleges are reluctant to send their
students to the Au Sable Institute for fear they will be "indoctrinated" with evolutionary theory. Au Sable tries to avoid discussions about "origins," as they call it, preferring to emphasize what
they view as a more significant concern, humanity's responsibility
to care for the earth, no matter how long it has been here. Still,
Mahan was able to tick off the evangelical schools that hold to a
doctrinaire "young earth" position and therefore discourage their
students from participating in the institute's programs.[11]

"I'm not an environmental nut or anything," one student told
me at the beginning of the term, emphasizing that he was at Au
Sable only to fulfill a course requirement. A day or two into the session, however, his suspicions had begun to dissipate. "I see God
working in nature," Jamie Heitzenrater of Emporium, Pennsylvania, said. "God put it here for a reason, and it's our duty to take
care of it."

In 2004, the National Association of Evangelicals, which customarily marches in lockstep with the Religious Right, issued a statement entitled "For the Health of the Nations." The very existence
of this document suggests that evangelicals finally may be coming

around on environmental matters. Among its points, the declaration lists several "degradations of creation," including deforestation, species extinction, and global toxification, calling on evangelicals to reflect more deeply "on the wonders of God's creation and the principles by which creation works." "We affirm that God-given dominion is a sacred responsibility to steward the earth and not a license to abuse the creation of which we are a part," the statement reads. "Because clean air, pure water, and adequate resources are crucial to public health and civic order, government has an obligation to protect its citizens from the effects of environmental degradation."[12] In contrast to the Religious Right signatories of the Cornwall Declaration, who persist in their efforts to discredit global warming, the evangelical magazine *Christianity Today* has acknowledged the crisis. The magazine also called on evangelicals to "make it clear to governments and businesses that we are willing to adapt our lifestyles and support steps towards changes that protect our environment." The Evangelical Environmental Network garnered a great deal of publicity with its "What Would Jesus Drive?" campaign against gas-guzzling automobiles in 2003. The organization, formed in 1994 by evangelicals like Calvin B. DeWitt, a professor of environmental studies at the University of Wisconsin who recently retired as dean of the Au Sable Institute, insists that "fuel economy and pollution from vehicles are serious moral issues."

This emerging environmental consciousness allows evangelicals once again to claim the mantle of a counterculture, a status they all but surrendered in the 1980s. It means standing against reckless corporate interests and the wholesale despoiling of God's creation. It means summoning the courage to refute the babble about New Age or neopagan entanglements no less than the cynicism of wise use propaganda or the defeatism of dispensationalism. Care for the created order also entails resistance to the dominant culture of consumerism, the overwhelming tendency to view resources as commodities.

No one I talked with at the Au Sable Institute was prepared to claim credit for the awakening of an environmental conscience among evangelicals. Most realize that environmental awareness lags far behind abortion or homosexuality on the political agenda for those associated with the Religious Right. "Most conservative Christians just don't get it," Dave Mahan lamented. Chris Newman chalks the lack of evangelical passion on environmental issues up to simple ignorance, though he uses the term descriptively and not as an indictment. "I have students who take my classes at Spring Arbor," he said, "who tell me later that this should be a required course."

The entrenched leaders of the Religious Right, however, will not surrender easily, as indicated by their attempts to intimidate evangelical environmentalists. In February 2006, a group of eighty-six evangelical leaders issued the "Evangelical Climate Initiative." "Our commitment to Jesus Christ," the statement reads, "compels us to solve the global warming crisis." Those signing the statement included thirty-nine presidents of evangelical colleges, including Duane Litfin of Wheaton College, and leaders of evangelical megachurches such as Rick Warren, pastor of Saddleback Church and author of *The Purpose-Driven Life*.

More conspicuous, however, were the names missing from the document: Ted Haggard, president of the National Association of Evangelicals, and Richard Cizik, the organization's vice president for governmental affairs. The National Association of Evangelicals had issued the earlier, 2004 declaration of concern for the environment, "For the Health of the Nation," at which time Cizik made a remarkable statement to the *New York Times.* "I don't think that God is going to ask us how he created the earth," Cizik said, "but he will ask us what we did with what he created."

In January 2006, however, prior to the release of the "Evangelical Climate Initiative," twenty-two prominent leaders of the Religious Right sent a letter to the National Association of Evangelicals demanding that the organization back away from environmental issues. "We have appreciated the bold stance that the National Association of Evangelicals has taken on controversial issues like embracing a culture of life, protecting traditional marriage and family," the letter read, but it implored the National Association of Evangelicals "not to adopt any official position on the issue of global climate change." Signatories to the letter included Charles Colson, Donald Wildmon, Richard Land, James Dobson, and Lou Sheldon, head of the Traditional Values Coalition.

Although Haggard and Cizik capitulated to pressure from these leaders of the Religious Right, the good news is that eighty-six other evangelicals refused to do so. Signing on to the "Evangelical Climate Initiative," with its call for legislation to reduce greenhouse emissions, hardly qualifies as a profile in courage, perhaps, but it suggests a crack in the alliance between evangelicals and hard-right, pro-business conservatives.

Care for the earth, God's creation, should be an instinctive response on the part of those who number themselves among the followers of Jesus—and even more so for those who insist that an intelligent designer fashioned the natural world. The Religious

Right, however, conjuring the goblins of neopaganism, have cast their lot with corporate and business interests, distorting the faith with a narrow, pinched reading of Genesis. This theology of dominion, coupled with the wise use ideology of corporate interests, places humanity in the role of exploiter and justifies the plundering of natural resources.

An increasing number of evangelicals, however, dissent from this rapacious ideology. They have decided to heed their consciences rather than obey the patter of the Religious Right. "I'm tired of those old white guys telling us what to think and do," a Christian college president and one of the signatories to the "Evangelical Climate Initiative" declared. It is here, on the issue of the environment, that maybe, just maybe, the Religious Right will lose its hammerlock on America's evangelicals, who in turn will summon the courage to reclaim the faith from hard-right zealots. The religious and political effects of that reclamation could be seismic.

As with any such movement, however, education is crucial, for it is the coming generation who will shape the future. The advocates of "school choice" and the founders of Patrick Henry College understand that very well, so they are working hard to undermine public education and to place ideologues strategically throughout society, especially in government. But evangelical attitudes on the environment suggest the presence of a countercurrent of young evangelicals willing to confront the distortions of the Religious Right. Although its students are small in number, the Au Sable Institute plays an important role in shaping the future.

Meghan Donaghue, one of the participants in the Au Sable winter term, provides an example. She has always loved the outdoors, so she came to Au Sable to learn more about the environment. "I used to be the biggest tree-hugger," she told me during a hike around Big Twin Lake. Though she now envisions working on other social-justice issues, especially forced prostitution in India, she vows never to neglect environmental concerns. "If you let it slip your mind, then you become like the world," she said. "And that's why we're here—to try to change the world."

Conclusion

Taking the Country Back

*These people come near to me with their mouth and
honor me with their lips, but their hearts are far
from me.*

ISAIAH 29:13

IN NOVEMBER 2002, THIRTY YEARS AFTER MY previous visit to
Wheaton College to hear George McGovern, I approached the
podium in Edman Chapel to address the student body. At evangelical colleges like Wheaton (and like the one I had attended up
the road), there are two kinds of required gatherings: chapel and
convocation. The former is religious in nature, whereas a speaker
at convocation has the license to be far more discursive, even
secular—or political. The college's chaplain, however, had invited
me to preach in chapel, not convocation, and so, despite the temptation, I delivered a homily about discerning God's will that was, as
I recall, not overly long, appropriate to the occasion, and reason-
ably well received.

I doubt very much that I will be invited back to Edman Chapel.
One of the benefits of being reared within evangelicalism, I suppose, is that you understand the workings of the evangelical subculture. I know, for example, that when this book appears, the minions
of the Religious Right will seek to discredit me, rather than engage

the substance of my arguments. The initial wave of criticism, as an old friend who has endured similar attacks reminded me, will be to deny that I am, in fact, an evangelical Christian. When that fails—and I'll put up my credentials as an evangelical against anyone!—the next approach will be some gratuitous personal attack: part of the academic elite, spokesman for the northeastern establishment, misguided liberal, prodigal son, traitor to the faith, or some such. Another evangelical friend with political views similar to mine actually endured a heresy trial.

To take another example, I've been an (unpaid) editor for *Christianity Today*, the signature publication of evangelicalism, for the better part of a decade and have written a dozen articles for them, including half a dozen features and several cover stories. A couple of years ago, the managing editor tried to pressure me into resigning from the masthead because I had agreed to address a group of gay evangelicals and because of a piece I had written challenging Religious Right orthodoxy on the abortion issue. I refused to oblige him by tendering my resignation then, but now, with the appearance of this book, he has the material he needs to force my ouster.[1]

The evangelical subculture, which prizes conformity above all else, doesn't suffer rebels gladly, and it is especially intolerant of anyone with the temerity to challenge the shibboleths of the Religious Right. Despite their putative claims to the faith, the leaders of the Religious Right are vicious toward anyone who refuses to kowtow to their version of orthodoxy, and their machinery of vilification strikes with ruthless, dispassionate efficiency. Longtime friends (and not a few family members) will shuffle uneasily around me and studiously avoid any sort of substantive conversation about the issues I've raised in this book—then quietly strike my name from their Christmas card lists. That's how the evangelical subculture operates. Circle the wagons. Brook no dissent.

I understand that. Just as I understood full well what was at stake when I clutched the lectern at Edman Chapel that blustery morning in November several years ago. And so, since my chances of being invited back to Edman Chapel, given the machinations of the subculture and the pressure for conformity, have dropped from slim to none, I offer here an outline of what I would like to say to the students at Wheaton and, by extension, to evangelicals everywhere.

Evangelicals have come a long way since my earlier visit to Edman Chapel in October 1972. We have moved from cultural obscurity, almost invisibility, to become a major force in American society. Jimmy Carter's run for the presidency launched us into the national consciousness in the mid-1970s. But evangelicals abandoned Carter by the end of the decade as the nascent Religious Right forged an alliance with the Republican Party and politically conservative evangelicals.

In terms of cultural and political influence, this alliance has been a bonanza for both sides. The Republican–Religious Right coalition dominates talk radio and controls a growing number of state legislatures and local school boards. They are seeking, with some initial success, to recast Hollywood and the entertainment industry. The Republicans have come to depend on Religious Right voters as their most reliable constituency, and, with the Republicans firmly in command of all three branches of the federal government, leaders of the Religious Right now enjoy unprecedented access to power.

And what has the Religious Right done with its political influence? Judging by the platform and the policies of the Republican Party—and I'm aware of no way to disentangle the agenda of the Republican Party from the goals of the Religious Right—the purpose of all this grasping for power looks something like this: an expansion of tax cuts for the wealthiest Americans, the continued prosecution of a war in the Middle East that has enraged our longtime allies and would not meet even the barest of just-war criteria, and a rejigging of Social Security, the effect of which, most observers agree, would be to fray the social safety net for the poorest among us. Public education is very much imperiled by Republican policies, to the evident satisfaction of the Religious Right, which seeks to replace science curricula with theology, thereby transforming students into catechumens.[2]

America's grossly disproportionate consumption of energy continues unabated, prompting demands for oil exploration in environmentally sensitive areas. The Bush administration has jettisoned U.S. participation in the Kyoto Protocol on climate change, which called on Americans to make at least a token effort to combat global warming. This administration has taken extraordinary steps to silence a government official who warns of the dangers of global warming. Corporate interests—Halliburton, Wal-Mart, Exxon-Mobil—are treated with the kind of reverence and deference once reserved for the deity.[3]

The Bible contains something like two thousand references to the poor and the believer's responsibility for the poor. Sadly, this obligation seems not to have trickled down into public policy. A single parent with two children in West Virginia, working forty hours a week at the federally mandated minimum wage, earns only $10,712 a year, well below the poverty level of $16,090. More likely than not, her full-time employment does not include health benefits. The number of American children below the poverty line has increased 12 percent since George W. Bush took office in 2001. An analysis of tax returns for the year 2003, on the other hand, revealed that Americans with an annual income of $1 million or more—approximately one-tenth of 1 percent of the taxpayers—reaped 43 percent of the savings from tax cuts on investment income.[4]

On judicial matters, judging by the nomination and confirmation of Samuel Alito to the U.S. Supreme Court, the Religious Right demands appointees who will diminish individual rights to privacy with regard to abortion. At the same time, if the support for Alito is any indication, the Religious Right approves a corresponding expansion of presidential powers, thereby disrupting the constitutionally mandated system of checks and balances that has served us so well for more than two centuries. Aside from the egregious Cleveland school voucher decision (*Zelman v. Simmons-Harris*) in 2002, the Supreme Court has, for the most part, kept the theocrats of the Religious Right at bay, but often by a slender margin. Alito's confirmation alters that equation.[5]

This Republican administration has justified the torture of human beings, God's creatures—some guilty of crimes, others not—on the basis of a memorandum written by a man who regards the Geneva Conventions as "quaint." On February 7, 2002, Bush issued an executive order declaring that "none of the provisions of Geneva apply to our conflict with Al Qaeda in Afghanistan or elsewhere throughout the world." The author of the rationale for the use of torture now serves as attorney general of the United States, the Cabinet official charged with safeguarding civil rights. This same administration believes that it is perfectly acceptable to conduct surveillance on American citizens without putting itself to the trouble of obtaining a court order, and it responds petulantly, even defiantly, to those who expose its illegal activities.

Indeed, the chicanery, the bullying, and the flouting of the rule of law that emanates from the nation's capital these days make Richard Nixon look like a fraternity prankster.

Where does the Religious Right stand in all this? Following the revelations that the U.S. government engaged in something the administration calls "extraordinary rendition," the exporting of prisoners to nations that have no scruples about the use of torture, I wrote to several prominent Religious Right organizations. Please send me, I asked in a straightforward message, a copy of your organization's position on this administration's use of torture. Surely, I thought, this is one issue that will allow the Religious Right to demonstrate its independence from this Republican administration, for surely no one who calls himself a child of God or who professes to hear "fetal screams" could possibly countenance the use of torture. Although I didn't really expect that the leaders of the Religious Right would climb out of the Republican Party's cozy bed over the torture of human beings, I thought perhaps they might poke a foot out from beneath the covers and maybe wiggle a toe or two.[6]

I was wrong. Of the eight Religious Right organizations I contacted, only two, the Family Research Council and the Institute on Religion and Democracy, answered my query. Both were eager to defend administration policies. "It is our understanding, from statements released by the Bush administration," the reply from

the Family Research Council read, "that torture is already prohibited as a means of collecting intelligence data." The Institute on
Religion and Democracy stated that "torture is a violation of human dignity, contrary to biblical teachings," but the organization's
president conceded that they had "not yet produced a more com-
prehensive statement on the subject," even months after the revelations. He worried that the "anti-torture campaign seems to be
aimed exclusively at the Bush administration," thereby creating a
public-relations challenge: The "impression is a real problem that
needs to be addressed."[7]

I'm sorry, but the use of torture *under any circumstances* is a
moral issue, not a public-relations dilemma. Amnesty International
has documented numerous cases of ill-treatment and torture at
U.S. facilities in Guantánamo Bay, Iraq, and Afghanistan. Tactics
include prolonged sleep deprivation, starvation, stress positions,
and severe beatings. Another favorite is a tactic called "waterboard-
ing," which entails submerging the captive in water to induce the
perception of drowning. Many, perhaps most, of the prisoners
taken in this administration's "war on terror" have not been
charged with any crime. In addition, under the policy of "extraordinary rendition," the government has sent prisoners to third
countries—Syria, Saudi Arabia, Egypt, and Uzbekistan—nations
that have been censured by the state department itself for their use
of torture.

Consider the case of Maher Arar, a Canadian citizen born in
Syria. On September 26, 2002, U.S. authorities took him into cus-
tody at New York's John F. Kennedy Airport. He was chained and
shackled and accused of being "a member of a known terrorist organization." Under the administration's policy of "extraordinary

rendition," Arar was shipped off to Syria by way of Jordan, where he was confined to an underground, gravelike, rat-infested cell. He was tortured by his captors for ten months. "Not even animals could withstand it," Arar said later. The U.S. government could find no evidence to support its charge that Arar was a member of a terrorist organization. No charges were ever filed, and he was finally released, without so much as an apology.[8]

But the Religious Right apparently has nothing to say about the use of torture. On December 5, 2005, the secretary of state, Condoleezza Rice, issued the first of her brazen defenses of torture. That same day, I contacted two prominent evangelical leaders, both of whom I consider friends. I pleaded that "we as evangelicals desperately need to come up with a statement opposing this administration's policies (and actions) on torture." One of my correspondents brushed me off; the other didn't bother to respond.

And what about abortion, the issue that the Religious Right decided in the early 1980s was its signature concern? Since January 2003, the Republican–Religious Right coalition has controlled the presidency and both houses of Congress—indeed, the president, the speaker of the House, and the majority leader of the Senate all claim to be evangelical Christians and unequivocally opposed to abortion—yet this coalition, curiously, has not tried to outlaw abortion. Why? Could it be that they are less interested in actually reducing the incidence of abortion (in which case, they should seek to alter public opinion on the matter) than they are in continuing to use abortion as a very potent political weapon, one guaranteed to mobilize their base and get out the vote?[9]

Equally striking as the agenda itself is the rhetoric that leaders of the Religious Right use to motivate their followers. In the course of these travels, I was impressed anew by the pervasiveness of the language of militarism among leaders of the Religious Right. Patrick Henry College, according to Michael Farris, "is training an army of young people who will lead the nation and shape the culture with biblical values." Rod Parsley, pastor of World Harvest Church in Ohio, issues swords to those who join his Religious Right organization, the Center for Moral Clarity, and calls on his followers to "lock and load" for a "Holy Ghost invasion." The Traditional Values Coalition advertises its "Battle Plan" to take over the federal judiciary. "I want to be invisible. I do guerilla warfare," Ralph Reed famously declared about his political tactics in 1997. "I paint my face and travel at night. You don't know it's over until you're in a body bag. You don't know until election night." The Family Research Council tries to enlist evangelicals to "fight the battle" against a "powerful alliance of leftists." And in Longview, Texas, I heard the strains of triumphalism: "The army of God is taking America back!" I wonder how this sounds in the ears of the Prince of Peace.[10]

This rhetoric and these policies are a scandal, a reproach to the gospel I honor and to the Jesus I love.

I went to Sunday school nearly every week of my childhood, and I have somewhere a pin recognizing perfect attendance for several consecutive years. But I must have been absent the day they told us that the followers of Jesus were obliged to secure even greater economic advantages for the affluent, to deny those Jesus called "the least of these" a living wage, and to despoil the environment by sacrificing it on the altar of free enterprise. I missed the lesson telling me that I should turn a blind eye to the suffering of others, even those designated as my enemies.[11]

The Bible I read says something quite different. It tells the story of ancient Israel's epic struggle against injustice and bondage—and of the Almighty's investment in the outcome of that struggle. But the Hebrew scriptures also caution against the imperiousness of this people, newly liberated from their oppressors, lest they treat others the way they themselves were treated back in Egypt. The prophets enjoin Yahweh's chosen people to "act justly and to love mercy and to walk humbly with your God" and warn of the consequences of failing to do so: exile and abandonment. "Administer true justice," the prophet Zechariah declares on behalf of the Lord Almighty, "show mercy and compassion to one another. Do not oppress the widow or the fatherless, the foreigner or the poor. Do not plot evil against each other."[12]

The New Testament echoes those themes, calling the followers of Jesus to care for orphans and widows, to clothe the naked, and to shelter the homeless. The New Testament I read says that, in the eyes of Jesus, there is no preference among the races and no distinction between the sexes. The Jesus I try to follow tells me that those who take on the role of peacemakers "will be called the children of God," and this same Jesus spells out the kind of behavior that might be grounds for exclusion from the kingdom of heaven: "I was hungry and you gave me nothing to eat, I was thirsty and you gave me nothing to drink, I was a stranger and you did not invite me in, I needed clothes and you did not clothe me, I was sick and in prison and you did not look after me."[13]

We could have a lively discussion and even vigorous disagreement over whether it is incumbent upon the *government* to provide these services, but those who argue against such measures should be prepared with some alternative program or apparatus. Even so, all but the most callous and obdurately ideological readings of the scriptures would make it difficult to support the torture of human beings, the denial of affordable health care, or the further enrichment of the wealthiest Americans at the expense of those less fortunate. The agenda of the Republican–Religious Right coalition, moreover, is utterly inconsonant with the distinguished record of evangelical activists in the nineteenth century. They interpreted the teachings of Jesus to mean that, yes, they really did bear responsibility for those on the margins of society, especially for the emancipation of slaves and for the rights of women. "I think the equality of men and women under the Gospel was one of the great principles that was to be announced by the apostles," an evangelical preacher declared in the nineteenth century.[14]

In addition to having distorted the teachings of Jesus, the Religious Right has also been cavorting with some rather unsavory characters in its quest for political and cultural power. Randy "Duke" Cunningham earned a 100 percent approval rating from Pat Robertson's Christian Coalition while a member of the House of Representatives. He resigned on November 28, 2005, after pleading guilty to accepting $2.4 million in bribes from defense contractors; Cunningham was sentenced to eight years in prison.

Time after time in the course of researching this book, I heard leaders of the Religious Right extol the Christian virtues of Tom DeLay, the "patronage saint" of the Republican Party and the ethically challenged majority leader of the House of Representatives who was forced to surrender his leadership post after his indictment on charges of criminal conspiracy. Just prior to DeLay's announcement that he would resign from Congress, Rick Scarborough compared

DeLay's legal struggles to the crucifixion of Jesus. Tom Coburn, an obstetrician and the junior U.S. senator from Oklahoma, was bedeviled during his 2004 campaign for the Senate by reports that he had sterilized a twenty-year-old woman without her consent and then filed a fraudulent claim for government reimbursement. Coburn has called for the death penalty for doctors who perform abortions.

For the better part of three decades now, we've been treated to the moral sermonizing of William J. Bennett, who wrote *The Book of Virtues* and served as Ronald Reagan's secretary of education and was one of Bill Clinton's most relentless critics. We now know that Bennett is a compulsive gambler, having lost something like $8 million in various casinos. Rush Limbaugh, who has attained almost iconic status in the eyes of many people sympathetic with the Religious Right, has acknowledged his addiction to prescription drugs and has allegedly tapped into a black market drug ring to supply his habit.

Ralph Reed, formerly the head of the Christian Coalition and currently a Republican candidate for lieutenant governor of Georgia, his first step on the road to the White House, has always preached against gambling as part of his "family values" rhetoric. Reed, who has also done consulting work for Enron (which engaged in other forms of gambling), accepted as much as $4.2 million from Indian tribes intent on maintaining a regional monopoly for their casinos. "I need to start humping in corporate accounts," he wrote to lobbyist Jack Abramoff, who has since pleaded guilty to federal charges of fraud, tax evasion, and conspiracy to bribe public officials. Reed added, "I'm counting on you to help me with some contacts."[15]

As head of the Republican Party in Georgia, Reed helped to engineer attacks on behalf of Saxby Chambliss in 2002 that accused Max

Cleland, the incumbent U.S. senator, of a lack of patriotism; Cleland left three of his limbs on the battlefields of Vietnam. As a political consultant for various Republican candidates, Reed has compiled a tawdry record of race-baiting, but he is far from alone among the ranks of the Religious Right in his questionable attitudes about race. Tony Perkins, a graduate of Jerry Falwell's Liberty University and head of the Family Research Council, arguably the most influential Religious Right organization aside from Focus on the Family, has had ties to white supremacist organizations in his native Louisiana.[16]

The purpose in ticking off this roll call of rogues associated with the Religious Right (and the list could have been longer) is not to single individuals out for obloquy and certainly not to suggest the absence of moral failings on the other side of the political spectrum—though I must say that some of this behavior makes Bill Clinton's adolescent dalliances pale by comparison. The point, rather, is to argue that those who make it their business to demand high standards of moral rectitude from others ought to be able to approach those standards themselves.

Too often, the leaders of the Religious Right confuse morality with moralism. A moralist takes it upon himself to stand in judgment, to point fingers at the shortcomings of others. Jesus had strong words for the moralists of his day, the religious leaders who were always tut-tutting about someone else's transgression, all the while neglecting the larger mandate of godliness, which Jesus reckoned in terms of compassion rather than judgment. He called them "blind guides," and he suggested that the faith of a repentant sinner was far superior to that of the moralist. "Why do you look at the speck of sawdust in someone else's eye," Jesus asked, "and pay no attention to the plank in your own eye?"[17]

My evangelical theology tells me that we are, all of us, sinners and flawed individuals. But it also teaches the importance of confession, restitution, and amendment of behavior—whether it be an adulterous tryst, racial intolerance, or prevarication in the service of combating one's enemies. We have seen nothing of the sort from these putatively Christian powerbrokers.

"Do not be misled," St. Paul wrote to the Corinthians. "'Bad company corrupts good character.'" Jesus himself asked, "What good would it be for you to gain the whole world, yet forfeit your soul?"[18]

The Religious Right has compromised the faith in other ways. The rise of the Religious Right has led many evangelicals to identify the cause of Christ with the agenda and the fortunes of the Republican Party. That is blasphemy, pure and simple, but it is also a configuration that has led to a denigration of the faith. The early years of the Religious Right provide a case in point. The pursuit of political power and influence in the 1980s came at a fearsome price.

For most of the twentieth century, evangelicalism had existed primarily within its own subculture, one that protected individuals from the depredations of the world. It was an insular universe, and the world outside of the subculture, including the political realm, was corrupt and corrupting. Believers had better beware. Along about 1980, however, evangelicals, newly intoxicated with political power and cultural influence, began to let down their guard. They succumbed to the seductions of the culture. It was during the Reagan years that we began to hear about the so-called prosperity gospel, the notion that God will reward true believers with the emoluments of this world. Evangelicalism was still a subculture in the 1980s, but it was no longer a counterculture. It had lost its edge, its capacity for cultural critique, because it had become al-most inseparable from the prevailing culture, especially as defined by the Republican Party.

Since I started writing this book, a number of people have asked me what the Religious Right wants. What would America look like if the Religious Right had its way? I've thought long and hard about that question in the course of my travels and my research, and the best answer that I can come up with is that the Religious Right han-kers for the kind of homogeneous theocracy that the Puritans tried to establish in seventeenth-century Massachusetts. They would love nothing more than to take the country back to the seventeenth century and, in so doing, to impose their vision of a moral order on all of society.

The Puritans left England and crossed the Atlantic in the 1630s to construct what John Winthrop called a "city on a hill," an example to the rest of the world and to England in particular. The Puritans configured church and state so that they would be both coterminous and mutually reinforcing, but only one form of worship was permit-ted. Anyone who challenged the hegemony of Puritan orthodoxy faced the wrath of the state, with penalties ranging from expulsion (Roger Williams and Anne Hutchinson) to deportation (Quakers) to execution (Quakers and those accused of witchcraft).

Without question, Puritanism in seventeenth-century Massa-chusetts was a grand and noble vision, but it ultimately collapsed beneath its own weight, beneath the arrogance of its own preten-sions. By the middle of the seventeenth century, Puritanism had become ingrown and calcified, the founding generation unable to transmit their piety to their children. By the waning decades of the century, in the face of encroaching pluralism—Anglicans and Quakers—and the rise of a merchant class, the Puritan ministers of Massachusetts were making increasingly impassioned, frantic calls for repentance. What frightened the Puritan ministers of the seventeenth century—no less than the leaders of the Religious Right at the turn of the twenty-first century—was pluralism. Puritans grew apoplectic at the thought of Quakers or Anglicans or anyone else threatening their religious hegemony or their tidy theocracy.

Despite the best efforts of the Puritan clergy, spirituality in New England continued to languish into the eighteenth century. The tide began to turn when fresher and more energetic preachers entered the scene in the 1730s. These ministers—George Whitefield, Gilbert Tennent, Isaac Backus, and others—challenged the cozy relationship between church and state and thereby reinvigorated religion in New England. The force of their ideas and their assault on the status quo spread throughout the Atlantic colonies in an utterly transformative event known as the Great Awakening.

The lesson of New England was clear. Religion, as Roger Williams had argued back in the 1630s, functions best *outside* the political order, and often as a challenge to the political order. When it identifies too closely with the state, it becomes complacent and ossified, and efforts to coerce piety or to proscribe certain behavior in the interests of moral conformity are unavailing.

Thankfully, the founding fathers recognized the wisdom of Williams's formula for church and state and codified it into the First Amendment, the best friend that religion has ever had. The First Amendment was a concession to pluralism, and its guarantee of a "free market" of religion has ensured a salubrious religious marketplace unmatched anywhere in the world.

Unfortunately, some of the clergy in New England still refused to concede their prerogatives and surrender to the religious marketplace. Although the First Amendment ensured the "free exercise" of religion and prohibited the government from favoring any one religious group, the Congregationalists in Massachusetts and Connecticut clung stubbornly to their establishment status, not wanting to forfeit the tax subsidies afforded them by the state. From his post in Litchfield, Connecticut, Lyman Beecher resisted "the fall of the standing order" in Connecticut, fearing the collapse of Congregationalism. In 1820, however, a scant two years after Connecticut did away with state-subsidized religion (Massachusetts would follow suit in 1833, the last state to do so), Beecher was forced to repent. Although he and his fellow Congregationalist ministers had feared "that our children would scatter like partridges," the effect of disestablishment was quite the opposite. "Before we had been standing on what our fathers had done," Beecher recalled, "but now we were obliged to develop all our energy." After disestablishment, he wrote, "there came such a time of revival as never before."[19]

The leaders of the Religious Right, just like their Puritan and Congregationalist forebears, are frightened by pluralism. That's understandable, especially for a movement that propagates the ideology that America is—and always has been—a *Christian* nation. Pluralism is messy. It requires understanding, accommodation, and tolerance, especially if we hope to maintain some semblance of comity and social order. The Puritans hated pluralism, as did the Protestants of the nineteenth century in the face of Catholic immigrants from Ireland, Germany, and Italy. Changes to the immigration laws in 1965 brought to the United States new hues of ethnic and religious pluralism, a rich and diverse palette unimaginable to the Protestants of the 1950s, let alone to the Puritans of the 1650s. Ever since those changes to the immigration laws, the arrival of Asians and South Asians has altered the religious landscape of the United States. Muslim mosques, Hindu and Shintô temples, Buddhist stupas, and Sikh gurdwârâs now dot the countryside.

By the late 1970s, the leaders of the Religious Right felt their hegemony over American society slipping away; one reading of the Religious Right is that many evangelicals believed that their faith could no longer compete in this new, expanded religious marketplace. No wonder the Religious Right wants to renege on the First Amendment. No wonder the Religious Right seeks to encode its version of morality into civil and criminal law. No wonder the Religious Right wants to emblazon its religious creeds and symbols on public property. Faced now with a newly expanded religious marketplace, the Religious Right wants to change the rules of engagement so that evangelicals can enjoy a competitive advantage. Rather than gear up for new competition, as Beecher had done in nineteenth-century Connecticut, the Religious Right seeks to use the machinations of government and public policy to impose their vision of a theocratic order.

But the lesson of seventeenth-century Puritanism, the very theocratic model that the Religious Right so admires, is that such efforts come to naught. Far from something to be feared, pluralism is a good thing. It keeps religious groups from resting on their laurels—or their endowments, in the case of mainline Protestantism—and makes them competitive in the marketplace of ideas.

Ironically, the one movement that has exploited this situation to its advantage more than any other in this religious marketplace is evangelical Protestantism. Evangelicals understand almost instinctively how to speak the idiom of the culture, whether it be the open-air preaching of George Whitefield in the eighteenth century, the circuit riders and the camp meetings of the antebellum period, the urban revivalism of Billy Sunday at the turn of the twentieth century, or the use of radio and television by various preachers in the twentieth and twenty-first centuries.

America has been kind to religion, but not because the government has imposed religious faith or practice on its citizens. Quite the opposite: Religion has flourished because religious belief and expression have been voluntary, not compulsory. We are a religious people precisely because we have recognized the rights of our citizens to be religious in a different way from us, or even not to be religious at all. We are simultaneously a people of faith and citizens of a pluralistic society, one in which Americans believe that it is inappropriate, even oppressive, to impose the religious views of a minority—or even of a majority—on all of society. That is the genius of America, and it is also the reason that religion thrives here as nowhere else.

Although no group has profited more from the First Amendment and the disestablishment of religion in America than evangelicals, the Religious Right would love nothing more than to dismantle the First Amendment and enshrine evangelical values and mores as the law of the land. As I argued in my testimony as an expert witness in the Alabama Ten Commandments case, religion has prospered in this country precisely because the government has stayed out of the religion business. The tireless efforts on the part of the Religious Right to eviscerate the First Amendment in the interest of imposing its own theocratic vision ultimately demean the

faith even as it undermines the foundations of a democratic order
that thrives on pluralism.

Jesus himself recognized that his followers held a dual citizenship. "Give back to Caesar what is Caesar's," he said, "and to God
what is God's." Negotiating this dual status can be fraught with
complications, but it is incumbent upon responsible citizens of this
earthly realm to abide by certain standards of behavior deemed essential for the functioning of the social order. Much as I would like
all of my fellow Americans to be Christians or vegetarians or Democrats, I have no right to demand it. The canons of democracy
and America's charter documents guarantee that I can argue,
wheedle, and cajole, but I cannot coerce. And my right to offer my
ideas, convictions, and beliefs into the arena of public discourse
presupposes my willingness to extend the same courtesy to others.
By seeking to commandeer and to dominate the conversation,
however, the leaders of the Religious Right have failed to observe
even the most basic etiquette of democracy.[20]

Is there a better way? Yes, I think so. It begins with an acknowledgement that religion in America has always functioned best from the
margins, outside the circles of power, and any grasping for religious
hegemony in this pluralistic context ultimately trivializes and dimin-
ishes the faith. The Puritans of the seventeenth century learned that
lesson the hard way, as did the mainline Protestants of the 1950s, who
sought to identify their faith with the white, middle-class values of the
Eisenhower era. In both cases, it was the evangelicals who stepped in
and offered a corrective, a vibrant expression of the faith untethered to
cultural institutions that issued, first, in the Great Awakening and,
second, in the evangelical resurgence of the 1970s.

For America's evangelicals, reclaiming the faith would produce a social and political ethic rather different from that propagated by the Religious Right. Care for the earth and for God's creation provides a good place to start, building on the growing evangelical discontent with the rapacious environmental policies of the Republican–Religious Right coalition. Once thinking evangelicals challenge Religious Right orthodoxy on environmental matters, further challenges are possible.

A full-throated, unconditional denunciation of the use of torture, even on political enemies, would certainly follow. How can any disciple of Jesus countenance the use of torture on other human beings? Even more so, how can evangelicals, who profess such concern about the fundamental rights of unborn children, defend those policies? Indeed, the act of abortion itself, except in cases of incest or rape, is, at the very least, morally disquieting, but it should be viewed as part of a much larger nexus of concerns. Evangelicals opposed to abortion would be well advised to follow Catholic teaching a bit further on this issue. As early as 1984, Joseph Cardinal Bernardin, the late archbishop of Chicago, talked about opposition to abortion as part of a "seamless garment," which included other "life issues": care for the poor and feeding the hungry, advocacy for human rights, and unequivocal opposition to capital punishment. Surely the adoption of what Bernardin called a "consistent ethic of life" carries with it broader moral authority than opposition to abortion alone.

As for abortion itself, evangelicals should consider carefully where they invest their energies on this matter. Both sides of the abortion debate acknowledge that making abortion illegal will not stop abortion itself; it *will* make abortions more dangerous for the life and health of the mother. The other complication is legal and constitutional. Especially at a time when the government's surveillance activities are already intruding on the privacy and the civil liberties of Americans, we should consider carefully the wisdom of allowing the government to determine a matter properly left to a woman and her conscience.

I have no interest in making abortion illegal; I would like to make it unthinkable. That is, I believe that the most effective way to limit the incidence of abortion is to change the moral climate surrounding the issue through education or even through public-service campaigns similar to those that discourage smoking or drugs or alcohol and spousal abuse. That strategy, more than ineffectual laws that intrude on individual rights, would take us farther toward eliminating abortion.

Taking this broader approach to "life issues" would affect evangelical attitudes not only toward abortion and capital punishment but also toward matters related to race and to the poor. The social and economic policies of this nation seem to have created a permanent underclass. If evangelicals believe that God cares about the fate of a fetus, it shouldn't require a huge leap in logic to surmise that God also cares about people of color or prisoners or immigrants or those with an orientation other than heterosexual.

Finally, an evangelical social and political ethic would take into account the pluralistic context of American society and recognize the genius of the First Amendment. That requires respect for the canons of democracy and for the importance of public education to ensure the future of democracy in America. It acknowledges, for example, that the proper venue for the teaching of creationism or intelligent design is the home or the Sunday school classroom, not the science curriculum. It means refusing to identify the symbols of the faith—the Bible, prayer, the Decalogue—with the political order, for that only demeans and trivializes the faith. In short, our best hope for the recovery of an evangelical social and political ethic lies with the Baptists—*genuine* Baptists who recognize, along with Roger Williams, founder of the Baptist tradition in America, that the faith functions best independently of the political order.

Indeed, one of the hallmarks of this grand experiment of democracy in America has been its vigilance over the rights of minorities. Evangelicals should appreciate that, for they were once a minority themselves. But the leaders of the Religious Right prefer the exercise of political influence to impose their vision of moral order on the nation, a vision with only tangential connections to the scriptures they claim as their authority, an interpretation informed less by the good news of the gospel or the humility of true discipleship than by the ruse of selective literalism dictated by ideological passions.

Their ideology, laced as it is with the rhetoric of militarism, represents a betrayal of the faith. The shameless pursuit of affluence and power and political influence has led the Religious Right into shady alliances and has brought dishonor to the gospel.

Evangelicals need once again to learn to be a counterculture, much as they were before 1980, before they succumbed to the seductions of power. Evangelicals must stand against what St. Paul called the "principalities and powers" of this world. The early followers of Jesus were a counterculture because they stood apart from the prevailing order. A counterculture can provide a critique of the powerful because it is utterly disinterested—it has no investment in the power structure itself.[21]

Indeed, the most effective and vigorous religious movements in American history have identified with the downtrodden and have positioned themselves on the fringes of society rather than at the centers of power. The Methodists of the nineteenth century come to mind, as do the Mormons. In the twentieth century, pentecostalism, which initially appealed to the lower classes and made room for women and people of color, became perhaps the most significant religious movement of the century.

A counterculture identifies with those on the margins. Jesus felt more comfortable with lepers and prostitutes and tax collectors than he did with the rulers of society. That is the posture of a counterculture, and it is a posture more becoming to those who number themselves among the followers of Jesus than hankering after worldly influence.

Since beginning my travels, I've developed an even greater suspicion of the bloviating preachers of the Religious Right, those who have anointed themselves shepherds of the flock and the arbiters of morality. They have led their sheep astray from the gospel of Jesus Christ to the false gospel of neoconservative ideology and into the maw of the Republican Party. And yet, my regard for the flock and my respect for the integrity of rank-and-file evangelicals is undiminished. Ultimately, it is they who must recover the scandal of the gospel and rescue us from the depredations of the Religious Right.

I challenge my fellow believers to reclaim their birthright as evangelical Christians and examine the scriptures for themselves— absent the funhouse mirror distortions of the Religious Right. For those equal to the task, I suggest a form of shock therapy: juxtapose the Sermon on the Mount (Matthew 5–7), arguably the highest expression of Christian ethics, with the platform of the Republican Party. Would Jesus, who summoned his followers to be "peacemakers" and invited them to love their enemies, jump at the opportunity to deploy military forces, especially at the cost of so many civilian lives? How do we reconcile reckless consumerism and tax cuts for the affluent with Jesus' warnings against storing up "treasures on earth, where moth and rust destroy, and where thieves break in and steal"? Is the denial of equal rights to anyone— women or Muslims or immigrants or gays—consistent with the example of the man who healed lepers and paralytics and who spent much of his time with the cultural outcasts of his day?[22]

I suspect that when Jesus asked us to love our enemies, he probably didn't mean that we should torture or kill them. I doubt that the man who expressed concern for the tiniest sparrow would approve the systematic despoiling of the environment in the interest of corporate profits. Jesus calls his followers to a higher standard.

The Bible I read tells of freedom for captives and deliverance from oppression. It teaches that those who refuse to act with justice or who neglect the plight of those less fortunate have some explaining to do. But the Bible is also about good news. It promises redemption and forgiveness, a chance to start anew and, with divine help, to get it right. My evangelical theology assures me that no one, not even Karl Rove or James Dobson, lies beyond the reach of redemption and that even a people led astray can find their way home.

That sounds like good news to me. Very good news indeed.

Appendix

Decoding the Rhetoric of
the Religious Right

*The atomic bomb is a marvelous gift that was given
to our country by a wise God."*
—PHYLLIS SCHLAFLY IN *MOTHER JONES*

I FIRST WROTE ABOUT EVANGELICALISM AS A "subculture" in the mid-1980s, and one of the characteristics of a subculture is that it has its own language and mores, its own values, and even, as in the case of evangelicalism, its own constellation of celebrities. The Religious Right (arguably a subculture within the evangelical subculture) also has its own jargon, a coded language that may be confusing to those outside the movement. I offer here a brief glossary as an aid to understanding some of the rhetoric commonly used by the Religious Right.

CHRISTIAN

When leaders of the Religious Right (and evangelicals generally) use the term *Christian*, it has a considerably narrower meaning than it does for the larger population. The Religious Right identifies a Christian as an evangelical believer, one who has had some kind of conversion experience. More important, the term excludes many others who think of themselves as Christians, including Mormons, most mainline (theologically liberal) Protestants, and nearly all Roman Catholics, although the reflexive exclusion of Catholics from the designation *Christian* has abated markedly over the last several decades, in large part because of their cooperation with the Religious Right on political causes. Usually, however, when a leader of the Religious Right mentions *Christians* or *Christian schools*, he is referring specifically to evangelical Christians or to evangelical schools.

JUDEO-CHRISTIAN TRADITION

Whenever someone talks about the *Judeo-Christian tradition* or *Judeo-Christian values*, I strongly advise that you check for your wallet and carefully count your change; the odds are better than even that she or he is trying to pull something over on you. The *Oxford English Dictionary* first noted the appearance of the term in 1899, and as various scholars have demonstrated, the term *Judeo-Christian* became popular in the 1930s in opposition to the waves of fascism then engulfing Europe. Contrary to appearances, however, the primary effect of the term was exclusion rather than inclusion; that is, by enlarging the bounds of religious acceptability beyond Protestantism to include Catholicism and Judaism in the 1930s, this newly coined Judeo-Christian tradition sought to exclude all others—practitioners of Asian religions, Mormons, pentecostals, Jehovah's Witnesses, and the like—from the realm of "American" religion. More importantly, what was once a relatively progressive term in the 1930s evolved over several decades into a phrase that, in the hands of the Religious Right, has become a synonym with "Christian nation."[1]

Leaders of the Religious Right frequently invoke "the Judeo-Christian tradition" as a way of pressing their argument that this "Judeo-Christian tradition" deserves a place of honor in American society, even to the point of excluding most other religious expressions. No one would deny that most of the founders considered themselves Christians; Jews certainly were present in eighteenth-century America, but they did not play a significant role in framing the government of the new nation, and the notion of any meaningful alliance between Jews and Christians would not have occurred to either group. The other rhetorical purpose of using the term *Judeo-Christian* is to suggest, somewhat misleadingly, that American Jews support the agenda of the Religious Right. While it is true that the leaders of the Religious Right occasionally line up some conservative rabbi to lend his name to a letterhead or even to address a Religious Right gathering, few American Jews lie awake at night worrying about whether or not the Ten Commandments are posted on the walls of American courtrooms.[2]

GAY LIFESTYLE

For leaders of the Religious Right, the term *gay lifestyle* connotes their belief that homosexuality is volitional rather than genetic. Although most of the scientific and medical research does not support this position, the Religious Right persists in arguing that individuals *choose* to be homosexual and that, conversely, they can choose not to be homosexual. Several organizations supported by the Religious Right—Exodus International, for instance—seek to "cure" gays and lesbians of their homosexuality. They often cite examples of individuals who have been "delivered" of their gay and lesbian orientations and who now live happily in heterosexual relationships, having renounced the "gay lifestyle." The record, however, is at best uneven. Many "ex-gays" have relapsed, including several prominent leaders of the "ex-gay" movement. Ralph Blair, an evangelical psychotherapist and founder of Evangelicals Concerned, a support group for gay evangelicals, insists that in all his years of practice, he has never encountered any homosexual who has been "cured" of his or her homosexuality.

GAY AGENDA

Although the origins of this phrase are not entirely clear, Anita Bryant is probably the person most responsible for advancing the notion of a *gay agenda*. Bryant, a former Miss Oklahoma and second runner-up Miss America in 1959, became enraged when the Metropolitan Dade County Commission in Florida passed an ordinance requiring that qualified homosexuals be hired as teachers in parochial and private schools. Bryant responded with a campaign in 1977 to repeal the measure, crusading under the banner of her newly formed organization, the Save Our Children Federation (later renamed Protect America's Children). Bryant argued that homosexuality was a sin and that if gays and lesbians were allowed to flaunt their "deviant lifestyles," then the American family and the American way of life would disappear. "Homosexuals cannot reproduce—so they must recruit," she warned. "And to freshen their ranks, they must recruit the youth of America." And what better recruiting ground than schools?

The notion of a "gay" or "homosexual agenda" has become a rhetorical staple for other leaders of the Religious Right, who imply a carefully planned strategy that supposedly unites all gay-rights groups into some kind of sinister cabal. In 1996, for instance, Ralph Reed warned against efforts by "the organized liberal gay lobby to seek affirmative government promotion of their lifestyle by granting minority status to gays or teaching homosexuality to children in the schools." Early in 2005, James Dobson of Focus on the Family denounced the use of a cartoon figure, SpongeBob SquarePants, in a video because he was concerned "about the way in which those childhood symbols are apparently being hijacked to promote an agenda that involves teaching homosexual propaganda to children." The Religious Right also warns that, in addition to the strategy of "recruiting" schoolchildren, the "gay agenda" seeks to undermine marriage with its push for same-sex unions.[3]

JUDICIAL ACTIVISM AND STATES' RIGHTS

When I attended "Justice Sunday" at Highview Baptist Church outside of Louisville, Kentucky, on April 24, 2005, I heard a lot of rhetoric about *judicial activism* and *states' rights*. The purpose of the rally, attended by a couple thousand evangelicals and carried by closed-circuit television to other churches across the country, was to press the Senate to forswear filibusters on judicial nominations, thereby paving the way for the confirmation of several of George W. Bush's more ideological appointments to the federal bench and, eventually, to the Supreme Court. A succession of speakers, including Charles Colson, James Dobson, and Bill Frist, majority leader of the Senate (who had voted in favor of a filibuster against one of Bill Clinton's judicial nominees) railed against the use of the filibuster and decried the "judicial activism" being perpetrated against the interests of the Religious Right. "You have a court that is out of control," Dobson lamented, citing the Supreme Court's rulings against prayer in schools, the *Roe v. Wade* decision, and the ruling of lower courts against the posting of the Ten Commandments in public buildings.

The case against "judicial activism" in the rhetoric of the Religious Right goes something like this. Unlike state legislators or members of Congress, federal judges are appointed for life and, for that reason, are not directly accountable to the people. "Activist judges," however, take it upon themselves to review, and occasionally to overturn, laws passed by the elected representatives of the people. Although this is precisely the function assigned to the judiciary under the Constitution's balance-of-powers provisions, the Religious Right worries in particular about "judicial activists" reversing legislation against same-sex unions, for example, on the grounds that such restrictive legislation violates the "equal protection under law" provision of the Fourteenth Amendment. When spokesmen for the Religious Right castigate "judicial activism," they often cite the example of the Warren Court, with its *Miranda* ruling (requiring police to apprise suspects of their rights), or the landmark *Brown v. Board of Education* decision of 1954, which mandated the desegregation of public schools.

A corollary to the Religious Right's condemnation of "judicial activism" is the assertion of states' rights. The argument here is that individual states should be able to decide matters for themselves without interference from the federal government. But this, too, is coded language, the vocabulary of racism and segregation in decades past.[4]

Until the federal judiciary stepped in, state courts and legislatures in the South routinely frustrated justice for lynching victims and for civil rights activists. Members of the Ku Klux Klan and other white supremacist organizations, such as the White Citizens' Councils, operated with impunity because they knew that the chances they would be prosecuted by local officials were negligible and that they would be convicted by a local jury were even smaller. The murderers of Emmett Till in Money, Mississippi, to cite one example of many, were acquitted by a white jury within minutes, even though the two men readily, even gleefully, admitted their crime several weeks later. George Wallace, governor of Alabama, invoking the principle of states' rights, refused to admit African Americans to the University of Alabama; one of the prominent planks in his platform when he ran for president in 1968 was states' rights. Only when the federal government stepped in (including "activist judges") were civil rights protesters able to gain any ground in their struggle for racial equality.

Tony Perkins, the principal organizer of "Justice Sunday," is well familiar with the coded language of "judicial activism" and "states' rights." Perkins was elected to the Louisiana House of Representatives in 1996, the same year he managed the U.S. Senate campaign of his friend Woodie Jenkins. In the course of the campaign, Perkins purchased a mailing list for $82,500 from David

Duke, the former grand imperial wizard of the Ku Klux Klan who had run twice for statewide office. In 2001, Perkins addressed the Louisiana chapter of the white supremacist Council of Conservative Citizens, the successor to the White Citizens' Councils, which had mobilized against Martin Luther King Jr. and civil rights activists during the struggle for civil rights. Perkins's own campaign for the U.S. Senate in 2002 was dogged by questions about his associations with Duke. He now heads the Family Research Council, one of the most powerful and prominent organizations of the Religious Right.[5]

Finally, when leaders of the Religious Right complain about judicial activism, they never mention *Bush v. Gore*, the Supreme Court decision that threw the disputed 2000 election to George W. Bush.

THE RHETORIC OF MARGINALITY

This is not so much a phrase as a rhetorical ploy, one that the Religious Right has exploited brilliantly for the past three decades. Leaders of the Religious Right persistently portray themselves and their followers as under attack by a variety of enemies—liberals, the Supreme Court, the American Civil Liberties Union, the "mainstream media," environmentalists, the "gay agenda," and any number of adversaries, real or imagined. "They are reluctant political actors," Ralph Reed said of politically conservative evangelicals. "Their way of life and their values are under assault." For better or worse, we live in a culture where the status of victim carries with it a certain cachet. That fact has not been lost on the leaders of the Religious Right.[6]

Despite the huge number of evangelicals in America and despite the overwhelming political muscle of the Religious Right—they now control all three branches of the federal government—leaders of the Religious Right continue to propagate this language of victimization. We are under siege, they warn. Our values are being attacked. Rick Scarborough repeatedly invokes the specter of "the judicial war on faith," and Tony Perkins warns that liberals are "determined to shut down the conservative movement in 2006 with a broad and relentless offensive—*against almost every value you and I cherish*." The accuracy of these protestations is questionable, but the rhetoric of marginality is undeniably effective in rallying support within the ranks of the Religious Right.[7]

Acknowledgements

As with all such projects, my debts are incalculable. In a very real sense, I owe the existence of this book to my sons. In the weeks following the 2004 elections, as I was vacillating between rage and despair, I kept recalling that my older son, Christian, had climbed aboard a bus in New York City in order to knock on doors in Ohio during the final weekend of the campaign. If he could do that, I chastened myself, then I could find a constructive way to channel my frustrations in the hopes of effecting some correction to this country's ruinous course. Andrew, my younger son, also has an Ohio connection. After graduation from high school in 2005, he elected to take a gap year and work for the AmeriCorps "City Year" program in the Cleveland public school system before joining his older brother as a student at Columbia. There are no words to convey how proud I am of both of my sons.

Virtually every time I lecture about the Religious Right to audiences around the country, someone asks what basis I have for hope rather than despair. My answer is simple: I'm a father, and the decision to become a parent is an expression of faith in the future. Put another way, because I have children, I don't have the luxury of despair.

Others have helped to shape my thinking about how people of faith function in this world. Any recitation of names is bound to produce omissions, but I cannot neglect to mention the formative influence of people like David Schlafer, Doug Frank, Sam Alvord, J. Edward Hakes, and the late Kenneth Shipps from my undergraduate days at Trinity College. John D. Woodbridge and Mark Noll were my first mentors as I began to study American religious history, although I suspect that neither will be entirely pleased with what I have argued here. The footnotes to this volume only begin to suggest the dimensions of my debt to John F. Wilson. I find it difficult to imagine any better educational venue than the religion department lounge at Princeton University in the early 1980s. There, graduate students could sip coffee and match wits with one another and with the likes of Jeffrey Stout and the late Paul Ramsey.

Students past and present have offered advice and encouragement on this project. Several have provided me with the benefit of their critical reading of portions of the manuscript: Lauren Winner, Jesse Todd, Shawn Landres, Sarah Cunningham, Rosemary Hicks, Erika Dyson, and Jodi Eichler-Levine. Members of the Columbia Seminar on Religion in America scrutinized an early draft of the first chapter, for which I am grateful. Adam Shapiro, who as an undergraduate took a seminar I taught on religion and science in the twentieth century, went on to doctoral studies at the University of Chicago; he provided helpful suggestions for the fourth chapter, based on his work on the Scopes trial.

As I was nearing the end of the editing process, I attended a conference at Michigan State University, sponsored by the Institute for the Study of Christianity and Culture. I should like to thank Malcolm Magee, the organizer of the event, for the invitation and for allowing me to try out some of these ideas. I'm also grateful to David W. Stowe, Robert Moore, and my colleague Amy DeRogatis

of Michigan State and to Corwin Schmidt of Calvin College for
their comments.

Laurel Kearns of Drew University and James Ball of the Evangelical Environmental Network helped me to navigate the chapter
on environmentalism, and Matthew Scully's excellent book, *Dominion: The Power of Man, the Suffering of Animals, and the Call
to Mercy,* was crucial to my thinking about the matter. James Dunn
of Wake Forest University, a *real* Baptist, read an early draft of the
second chapter and offered helpful suggestions, and Richard Pier-
ard of Gordon College confirmed my recollections of that remarkable gathering of Religious Right leaders in November 1990, the
conference that supplied me with the evidence I needed to expose
the abortion myth. I'm grateful also for the advice and the encouragement of my colleagues Alan Segal, Celia Deutsch, John Stratton
Hawley, Alan Gabbey, and Richard Pious.

Aside from the students themselves, one of the delights of being
a visiting professor at Yale Divinity School over the past couple of
years is grabbing a beer with Harry Stout (known to his friends as
"Skip") after class. He provided me with advice and friendship,
and he encouraged me not to shrink from my efforts to slay the
dragon of the Religious Right.

It should go without saying, but in this case, given the machinations of the Religious Right, the caveat is more than a formality: I
alone bear responsibility for the content and the arguments presented here. This book is an expression of my views, not those of
the people who have assisted me.

Lara Heimert, my editor, is superb—as is the entire staff at Basic
Books. This is my tenth (or so) book, but I've never had an editor
tangle with me over argument or the organization of ideas the way

she has. I'm grateful. The book is infinitely better because of her tireless efforts. I also want to acknowledge the support and encouragement of the late Liz Maguire.

Finally, as always, my greatest debt is to my matchless wife. Catharine is my companion and my best friend. She is a formidable scholar and a skilled interlocutor. I'd be lost without her. She has also demonstrated infinite patience and unstinting support during the writing of this book, even though she is convinced that agents for Fox News or the National Security Agency or Focus on the Family will come knocking.

By the way, lest I forget, I don't speak for her, either.

—HOLY SATURDAY
APRIL 15, 2006

Notes

PREFACE

1. On Bryan, see the excellent new biography by Michael Kazin, *A Godly Hero: The Life of William Jennings Bryan* (New York: Alfred A. Knopf, 2006).

2. Robertson quoted in William Martin, *With God on Our Side: The Rise of the Religious Right in America* (New York: Broadway Books, 1996), 166.

3. "Getting God's Kingdom into Politics," *Christianity Today*, September 19, 1980, 10 [1031].

4. The specific references are John 3:3 and 1 Peter 1:23.

5. Matthew 28:19–20 (Today's New International Version).

6. See Randall Balmer, *Mine Eyes Have Seen the Glory: A Journey into the Evangelical Subculture in America*, 4th ed. (New York: Oxford University Press, 2006); Randall Balmer, *Encyclopedia of Evangelicalism*, rev. ed. (Waco, TX: Baylor University Press, 2004). The *Princeton Religion Research Report*, released in 2002, for example, charts the number of Americans "describing self as born-again or evangelical" from 1976 through 2000. The percentages range from a low of 33 percent in 1987 and 1988 (during the televangelist scandals) to 47 percent in 1998. The percentage for 2000, the most recent year included in the Gallup figures, was 45 percent. Polling data are always problematic, of course, and one of the factors is that many Americans who fit the definition of *evangelical* (Southern Baptists, for instance) don't always recognize themselves by that term. The Institute for the Study of American Evangelicals, housed at the Billy Graham Center at Wheaton College, calculates that a *conservative* estimate of the number of evangelicals in America is 70 to 80 million, about 35 percent of the population.

7. For a fuller account of my spiritual and religious pilgrimage, see Randall Balmer, *Growing Pains: Learning to Love My Father's Faith* (Grand Rapids, MI: Brazos Press, 2001).

8. Balmer, *Mine Eyes Have Seen the Glory*, 342.

9. I consider McGovern, along with Jane Addams and Herbert Hoover, one of the three great American humanitarians of the twentieth century.

10. Some of the books that have shaped my understanding of evangelicalism in the nineteenth century include Timothy L. Smith, *Revivalism and Social Reform: American Protestantism on the Eve of the Civil War* (New York: Harper & Row, 1957); Norris A. Magnuson, *Salvation in the Slums: Evangelical Social Work,*

1865–1920 (Metuchen, NJ: Scarecrow Press, 1977); Donald W. Dayton, *Discovering an Evangelical Heritage* (New York: Harper & Row, 1976); Richard J. Carwardine, *Evangelicals and Politics in Antebellum America* (New Haven, CT: Yale University Press, 1993). For the narrative I have constructed here, Smith's book was formative; I recall that he spoke in chapel at Trinity College one day while I was a student there.

11. For the most part, I avoid the terms *fundamentalist* and *fundamentalism* in this book—not because they aren't useful, but because they are so frequently misused. The term *fundamentalism* derives from a series of pamphlets published between 1910 and 1915 by theologically conservative Protestants in an effort to stanch the drift toward liberalism in Protestant denominations. Those who subscribed to the doctrines set forth in these pamphlets (including the virgin birth of Jesus, the authenticity of miracles, and the inerrancy of the scriptures) came to be known as fundamentalists. The word has since been applied to other religious traditions—Hindu fundamentalists, Jewish fundamentalists, Mormon fundamentalists, Muslim fundamentalists—but the term belongs properly to American religious history. Fundamentalism has come to denote a kind of militancy, in addition to (in the American context) separatism and sectarianism. It applies to the Religious Right in that it tends to be relentlessly dualistic in its view of the world.

12. One very rough approximation of the organizations making up the Religious Right is a federation calling itself the Arlington Group (so named because one of its first meetings was in Arlington, Virginia). It was convened initially by Paul Weyrich in the mid-1990s and later by Don Wildmon of the American Family Association. Still, even that federation of about twenty organizations does not exhaust the institutional reach of the Religious Right.

13. In his sketch of the historical background of the Religious Right, George Marsden cites as one of the precedents what he calls a "Conscience Coalition," beginning in the antebellum period and extending into the twentieth century, but the politics of this movement, as he points out, would not generally be aligned on the right of the political spectrum. See George Marsden, "The Religious Right: A Historical Overview," chapter 1 in *No Longer Exiles: The Religious New Right in American Politics*, ed. Michael Cromartie (Washington, D.C.: Ethics and Public Policy Center, 1993).

Chapter 1

1. Laurie Goodstein and Greg Myre, "Clerics Fighting a Gay Festival for Jerusalem," *New York Times*, March 31, 2005, A1, A4.

2. For background information on the controversy, see Randal C. Archibold, "High on a Hill above San Diego, a Church-State Fight Plays Out," *New York Times*, October 1, 2005.

3. Jennifer Vigil, "Council Rescinds Decision on Cross," *San Diego Union-Tribune*, May 18, 2005, A1, A15.

4. Matthew 5:9 (TNIV).

5. Again, this is a theologically defensible position, based on the doctrine of human depravity (the idea that every human being inherits the sin of Adam), but the traditional understanding of depravity holds that Adam's sin is transmitted at the moment of conception, so presumably the fetus is not entirely innocent, in theological terms.

6. Randall Balmer, *Mine Eyes Have Seen the Glory: A Journey into the Evangelical Subculture in America*, 4th ed. (New York: Oxford University Press, 2006), 158.

7. Michael Luo, "On Abortion, It's the Bible of Ambiguity," *New York Times*, Week in Review, November 13, 2005, 1, 3. In our family, we refer to this kind of reasoning as the it's-the-vibe-of-the-thing argument, taken from a hilariously memorable scene in the movie *Castle*.

8. Malachi 2:16 (TNIV); Matthew 19:9 (TNIV); 1 Corinthians 7:11 (TNIV).

9. Matthew 5:32 (TNIV).

10. 1 Corinthians 11:4 (TNIV); 1 Timothy 2:12 (TNIV). See also 1 Corinthians 14:34, where Paul writes, "Women should remain silent in the churches" (TNIV).

11. It's not my task here to present a biblical case for or against homosexuality. The Religious Right has made the former argument copiously, basing its objections on passages taken from the Old and New Testaments. For alternate readings of those same passages, see David G. Meyers and Letha Dawson Scanzoni, *What God Has Joined Together? A Christian Case for Gay Marriage* (San Francisco: Harper San Francisco, 2005), ch. 7, and Peter T. Gomes, *The Good Book: Reading the Bible with Mind and Heart* (New York: William Morrow, 1996), ch. 8.

12. One of the best illustrations of the fundamentalist penchant for dualism is James Davison Hunter, *Culture Wars: The Struggle to Define America* (New York: Basic Books, 1991).

13. Employing a strict, literalistic approach to the Bible, the only warrant for divorce is marital infidelity.

14. For an example of this argument, see Michael Cromartie, ed., *No Longer Exiles: The Religious New Right in American Politics* (Washington, D.C.: Ethics and Public Policy Center, 1993), 75.

15. "Abortion and the Court," *Christianity Today*, February 16, 1973, 32 [502]; quoted in "What Price Abortion?" *Christianity Today*, March 2, 1973, 39 [565]; *Annual of the Southern Baptist Convention* (Nashville, TN: Executive Committee, Southern Baptist Convention, 1971), 72. This, admittedly, was before the 1979 fundamentalist takeover of the Southern Baptist Convention, but the convention could never in its history be described as liberal, except by the most partisan observer. Also, the convention's observation of the importance of church-state separation was the relic of an earlier age, before the Southern Baptist Convention ceased to be Baptist; see chapter 2. Quoted in "Abortion Decision: A Death Blow?" *Christianity Today*,

February 16, 1973, 48 [516]. William Martin, the most prominent historian of the Religious Right, writes about the aftermath of the *Roe* decision, "Evangelical and fundamentalist Protestants, many of whom now consider abortion a litmus test of extraordinary importance, had little to say about it one way or another" (*With God on Our Side: The Rise of the Religious Right in America* [New York: Broadway Books, 1996], 193).

16. Quoted in Martin, *With God on Our Side*, 172.

17. Quoted in Martin, *With God on Our Side*, 173. On the Bob Jones University case and the importance of schools to the formation of the Religious Right, see pp. 168–173.

18. Cromartie, *No Longer Exiles*, 26. This volume contains the published proceedings from the conference.

19. Cromartie, *No Longer Exiles*, 26; quoted in Martin, *With God on Our Side*, 173.

20. Cromartie, *No Longer Exiles*, 52. In the same comments, Dobson cites "government interference in Christian schools" as one of the reasons for the formation of the Religious Right and noted that this new movement "attempted to preserve the integrity of our organizations" (Cromartie, *No Longer Exiles*, 52).

21. I have since checked Weyrich's account with several leaders of the Religious Right, including Tim LaHaye. All of them confirm the substance of Weyrich's narrative, albeit somewhat reluctantly because it exposes the "abortion myth." Ralph Reed has also acknowledged the inaccuracy of the Religious Right's claim that evangelicals mobilized in direct response to *Roe v. Wade*, writing that "most evangelicals were slow to respond following the Supreme Court ruling" (*Active Faith: How Christians Are Changing the Soul of America Politics* [New York: Free Press, 1996], 216).

22. Quoted in Frances FitzGerald, *Cities on a Hill: A Journey through Contemporary American Cultures* (New York: Simon & Schuster, 1981), 29. The attempt to portray the Religious Right as the "new abolitionists" has not abated. The Family Research Council sent out an e-mail newsletter on April 6, 2005, which sought to make that parallel between the antiabortionists and the abolitionists.

23. Charles Colson, with Anne Morse, "A More Excellent Way," *Christianity Today* (February 2006): 144; Cromartie, *No Longer Exiles*, 55.

24. The *Griswold v. Connecticut* case was a challenge to an 1879 state law, which read, "Any person who uses any drug, medicinal article or instrument for the purpose of preventing conception shall be fined not less than fifty dollars or imprisoned not less than sixty days nor more than one year or be both fined and imprisoned." The Court ruled that the "statute forbidding use of contraceptives violates the right of marital privacy which is within the penumbra of specific guarantees of the Bill of Rights."

25. Quoted in "Abortion Decision: A Death Blow?" *Christianity Today*, February 16, 1973, 48 [516].

26. The Guttmacher Institute reports that 57 percent of women seeking abortions are "economically disadvantaged." See also Lawrence B. Finer and Stanley K. Henshaw,

"Estimates of U.S. Abortion Incidence in 2001 and 2002," Guttmacher Institute, New York City.

27. Interview with David Warnick, Rathdrum, Idaho, October 21, 2005.

28. Clinton's critics, with some justification, fault him for neglecting the final third of that formula, although the abortion rate dropped steadily during the 1990s. Some attribute that to the economic conditions during the Clinton years as compared with either Bush administration.

29. My colleague, Celia Deutsch, reminds me that the Catholic Church has issued a statement warning the faithful not to base their votes on a single issue.

30. The Court ruled in *Romer v. Evans* that a state "cannot so deem a class of persons a stranger to its laws." As one of my good friends, a gay man, said in response to this latter argument, given all the opprobrium that American society directs toward homosexuals, "Why would anyone *choose* to be gay?"

31. Jerry Falwell, *Listen, America!* (Garden City, NY: Doubleday, 1980), 183.

32. Jesus, I believe, was speaking eschatologically in John 17, the passage generally cited as the basis for ecumenism; the verb mood is subjunctive, not hortative. Yes, his followers will all be one, but not in this world, any more than the meek will inherit the earth. Also, Paul, the apostle, writes, "we know in part, and we prophesy in part." In the first letter to the Corinthians, moreover, Paul acknowledged that "some follow Paul and some follow Appollos," a passage that suggests to me a kind of nascent denominationalism as early as the first century.

33. Mainline Protestants sought, with limited success, to reclaim a prophetic mantle in the late 1950s and through the 1960s, especially with the civil rights movement and opposition to the war in Vietnam. They had so compromised themselves in the 1950s, however, that the younger generation had turned away.

34. I mean the question about Reagan as descriptive, not sardonic, although I do think it's ironic. I recall insistent denunciations of divorce throughout my evangelical childhood, and I remember asking my parents in the mid-1960s what they thought about Nelson Rockefeller. My mother replied unequivocally that Christians (read evangelicals) could never even think of voting for Rockefeller because he was divorced and remarried. Evangelicals were forced to reconsider their stand on the matter when so many of their own had divorced (and many remarried), but their embrace of Reagan accelerated the process so that the denunciations tailed off dramatically in the 1980s. Actually, divorce has for a long time been evangelicalism's dirty little secret. When I was writing my *Encyclopedia of Evangelicalism*, I was astonished to learn how many venerable evangelical leaders, including, for example, C. I. Scofield of the *Scofield Reference Bible*, had been divorced. (Scofield, in fact, had abandoned his wife and children before he was divorced.) See Randall Balmer, *Encyclopedia of Evangelicalism*, rev. ed. (Waco, TX: Baylor University Press, 2004), passim.

35. Matthew 22:37–39 (TNIV).

CHAPTER 2

1. On Monday, August 22, 2005, Robertson declared on his television program, "We have the ability" to assassinate Venezuelan president Hugo Chávez. "The time has come [to] exercise that ability." The U.S. government, he added, "ought to go ahead" and kill Chávez because "it's a whole lot cheaper than starting a war" (*USA Today*, August 24, 2005, 3A). In 1999, Robertson had called for the United States to change its foreign policy to permit the assassination of world leaders. "It would just seem so much more practical to have that flexibility," he said. "I just think it's the intelligent thing to do and I don't see anything un-Christian about it" (quoted in Rob Boston, "Guerillas and Bodybags and Sharks—Oh My! A Short History of Pat Robertson's Christian Coalition," *Church & State*, January 2002, 8).

2. Gohmert was one of the few members of Congress to oppose John McCain's amendment to outlaw the use of torture by the U.S. government. Gohmert called the McCain amendment "stupid."

3. I learned about Scarborough when we were guests together on National Public Radio's *The Connection* on June 24, 2005.

4. Louisiana Baptist Theological Seminary, not to be confused with New Orleans Baptist Theological Seminary, was founded in 1973 and bills itself as "a pioneer in distance education."

5. Quoted in John F. Wilson and Donald L. Drakeman, eds., *Church and State in American History: Key Documents, Decisions, and Commentary from the Past Three Centuries*, 3rd ed. (Boulder, CO: Westview Press, 2003), 21. Religious groups in other colonies also appealed for freedom of religious expression. On December 27, 1657, a group of Quakers living on Long Island issued the famous Flushing Remonstrance: "We desire therefore in this case not to judge least we be judged, neither to condemn least we be condemned, but rather let every man stand and fall to his own Master. Wee are bounde by the Law to Doe good unto all men, especially to those of the household of faith. And though for the present we seem to be unsensible of the law and the Law giver, yet when death and the Law assault us, if we have our advocate to seeke, who shall plead for us in this case of conscience betwixt God and our own souls; the powers of this world can neither attack us, neither excuse us, for if God justifye who can condemn and if God condemn there is none can justify."

6. Quoted in Wilson and Drakeman, *Church and State*, 30, 31.

7. Quoted in Edwin S. Gaustad, *Faith of the Founders: Religion and the New Nation, 1776–1826*, 2nd ed. (Waco, TX: Baylor University Press, 2004), 33. Gaustad's works on the topic provide probably the best summation of the understanding of church-state matters by the architects of the republic.

8. William G. McLoughlin, ed., *Isaac Backus on Church, State, and Calvinism: Pamphlets, 1754–1789* (Cambridge, MA: Harvard University Press, 1968), 315, 314. Italics in original.

9. Quoted in Wilson and Drakeman, *Church and State*, 59, 64.

10. Quoted in Wilson and Drakeman, *Church and State*, 69.

11. Quoted in Edwin S. Gaustad, *Proclaim Liberty throughout the Land: A History of Church and State in America* (New York: Oxford University Press, 1999), 27.

12. Forrest Church, ed., *The Separation of Church and State: Writings on a Fundamental Freedom by America's Founders* (Boston: Beacon Press, 2004), 92.

13. See Wilson and Drakeman, *Church and State*, 71.

14. Rachel Graves, "A Passion for Mixing Religion and Politics," *Houston Chronicle*, May 20, 2005. I presume that Scarborough subscribes to the other hallmark of the Baptist tradition, adult baptism, but given his utter disregard for liberty of conscience, I can't be sure.

15. Rick Scarborough, *In Defense of Mixing Church and State: A Call to Stand Up, Speak Up, and Refuse to Give Up* (Houston, TX: Vision America, 1999), 8–9. For a more extensive discussion of religion, the founders, and the separation of church and state, see some of the excellent work of Edwin S. Gaustad, for example, *Faith of the Founders: Religion and the New Nation, 1776–1826*, 2nd ed. (Waco, TX: Baylor University Press, 2004), and several books on Williams. I have also treated the First Amendment more thoroughly in Randall Balmer, *Blessed Assurance: A History of Evangelicalism in America* (Boston: Beacon Press, 1999), ch. 2.

16. Quoted in Wilson and Drakeman, *Church and State*, 87. Although the First Amendment called for disestablishment, several of the states retained their religious establishments into the early decades of the nineteenth century. Connecticut disestablished Congregationalism in 1818, and Massachusetts (the last state to do so) followed suit in 1833.

17. Some years ago, I was on a panel at Gordon College when one of the leaders of the Religious Right actually advocated a prescribed prayer from a different religion for every school day, a concession of sorts, I suppose, to religious pluralism.

18. Scarborough, *Mixing Church and State*, 9; quoted in Wilson and Drakeman, *Church and State*, 74.

19. Roger Williams, *The Bloudy Tenent of Persecution for Cause of Conscience*, ed. Richard Groves, with an introduction by Edwin Gaustad (Macon, GA: Mercer University Press, 2001), xxiv.

20. Scarborough, *Mixing Church and State*, 12.

21. Quoted in Wilson and Drakemam, *Church and State*, 21.

22. Quoted in Wilson and Drakemam, *Church and State*, 23, 22.

23. Curiously, however, when Moore filed his appeal with the Eleventh Circuit, he did not ask for a stay of Thompson's order to have the monument removed, a fairly routine request—and one routinely granted. Robert J. Varley, one of the lead attorneys for the plaintiffs, believes that Moore was spoiling all along for a confrontation.

24. Williams, *Bloudy Tenent*, 4.

25. Quoted in Wilson and Drakeman, *Church and State*, 75.

26. On Meese's role in popularizing this notion, see Lynette Clemetson, "Meese's Influence Looms in Today's Judicial Wars," *New York Times*, August 17, 2004, A1, A16.

27. Matthew 6:5 (TNIV); Randall Balmer, "John Henry Goetschius and 'The Unknown God': Eighteenth-Century Pietism in the Middle Colonies," *Pennsylvania Magazine of History and Biography* 113 (1989): 599.

28. Rousas John Rushdoony, *Thy Kingdom Come: Studies in Daniel and Revelation* (Fairfax, VA: Thoburn Press, 1978), 172.

29. Rushdoony, *Thy Kingdom Come*, 39, 194.

30. Quoted in Wilson and Drakeman, *Church and State*, 22.

Chapter 3

1. One of these volunteers was Andrew, my younger son, who elected to work for AmeriCorps during his gap year between graduating from high school and matriculating at Columbia.

2. "American Federation of Teachers Files Lawsuit against the State of Ohio over Cleveland School Voucher Program," *U.S. Newswire*, January 10, 1996.

3. Joining Rehnquist in the majority were Justices Antonin Scalia, Clarence Thomas, Anthony Kennedy, and Sandra Day O'Connor. Stephen G. Breyer, David Souter, Ruth Bader Ginsburg, and John Paul Stevens issued vigorous dissents.

4. Zach Schiller, "Cleveland School Vouchers: Where the Students Come From," report from Policy Matters Ohio, 2001, Cleveland and Columbus, Ohio.

5. Joe Hallett, "Self-appointed Superintendent," *Columbus Dispatch*, October 23, 2005.

6. Milton Friedman, "Public Schools: Make Them Private," *Washington Post*, February 19, 1995.

7. Hallett, "Self-appointed Superintendent." According to the newspaper, Brennan's family has contributed more than $3.8 million to Republicans since 1984; Voinovich, now one of Ohio's U.S. senators, has received more than $120,000.

8. Hallett, "Self-appointed Superintendent."

9. Cf. William Martin, *With God on Our Side: The Rise of the Religious Right in America* (New York: Broadway Books, 1996), 70–71.

10. Jerry Falwell, *Listen, America!* (Garden City, NY: Doubleday, 1980), 205.

11. Matthew 6:5–6 (TNIV).

12. The two cases at issue were *Engel v. Vitale* (1962) and *Abington Town School District v. Schempp* (1963).

13. Falwell, *Listen, America!* 205.

14. Quoted in Randall Balmer, *Mine Eyes Have Seen the Glory: A Journey into the Evangelical Subculture in America*, 4th ed. (New York: Oxford University Press, 2006), 171.

15. Corey Cutrer, "'Get Our Kids Out': Dobson Says Pro-Gay School Curriculum Has Gone Too Far," ChristianityToday.com, August 5, 2002.

16. "Dobson Again Calls for Parents to Pull Kids out of Public Schools," ChristianityToday.com, July 9, 2002. Dobson also mentioned Pennsylvania, Rhode Island, Hawai'i, and Alaska as promoting homosexuality.

17. Falwell, *Listen, America!* 218–219, 223.

18. Friedman, "Public Schools: Make Them Private."

19. Deborah Solomon, "School Monitor: Questions for Jonathan Kozol," *New York Times Magazine*, September 4, 2005, 14.

20. Remarks by Reg Weaver, vice president of the National Education Association, to the National Association for the Advancement of Colored People 90th Annual Convention, Labor Luncheon, July 13, 1999.

21. The school bestows the "Tim LaHaye Award for Leadership" and the "Beverly LaHaye Award for Leadership" annually to a male and a female student, respectively. In April 2006, the school announced that Farris would become chancellor and that Graham Walker would assume the duties of president.

22. For the record, Stevens was appointed to the U.S. Supreme Court in 1975 by Gerald R. Ford.

23. David D. Kirkpatrick, "College for the Homeschooled Is Shaping Leaders for the Right," *New York Times*, March 7, 2004.

24. The odd quotation about "the shining tip of the spear" appeared in a fundraising letter from the college, dated November 30, 2005.

25. Matthew 5:13–15 (TNIV).

CHAPTER 4

1. Quoted in Mark A. Noll et al., *Eerdmans' Handbook to Christianity in America* (Grand Rapids, MI: Wm. B. Eerdmans, 1983), 325. Regarding Protestant responses to Darwin, see Jon H. Roberts, *Darwinism and the Divine in America: Protestant Intellectuals and Organic Evolution, 1859–1900* (Madison: University of Wisconsin Press, 1988).

2. The best account of the Scopes trial is Edward J. Larson, *Summer for the Gods: The Scopes Trial and America's Continuing Debate over Science and Religion* (New York: Basic Books, 1997).

3. H. L. Mencken, "Battle Now Over, Mencken Sees Genesis Triumphant and Ready for New Jousts," *Baltimore Sun*, July 18, 1925; Mencken, "Tennessee in the Frying Pan," *Baltimore Sun*, July 20, 1925; Mencken, "Bryan," *Baltimore Sun*, July 27, 1925.

4. Regarding the construction of evangelical and fundamentalist institutions in the 1920s and 1930s, see Joel A. Carpenter, *Revive Us Again: The Reawakening of American Fundamentalism* (New York: Oxford University Press, 1997). For a glimpse into this

subculture in the decades surrounding the turn of the twenty-first century, see Randall Balmer, *Mine Eyes Have Seen the Glory: A Journey into the Evangelical Subculture in America*, 4th ed. (New York: Oxford University Press, 2006).

5. See Garry Wills, *Under God: Religion and American Politics* (New York: Simon & Schuster, 1990), ch. 9.

6. James C. Hefley, *Are Textbooks Harming Your Children?* (Milford, MI: Mott Media, 1979), 33.

7. As Adam Shapiro pointed out to me, the implications of *McLean* also prefigured an important strategy for the intelligent-design crowd. The judge, William R. Overton, ruled that creation science is a religion because it's not a science. Because the ruling placed the two in direct opposition, the proponents of intelligent design must demonstrate both that it is a science and that it is not a religion.

8. Phillip E. Johnson, *Darwin on Trial* (Washington, D.C.: Regnery Gateway, 1991). The notion of intelligent design certainly preceded Johnson's entry into the debate over origins, but he has given it a legitimacy it probably would not have attained otherwise. William A. Dembski, whom I shall introduce later in this chapter, writes, "Phil Johnson is the de facto leader of the intelligent design movement" (William Dembski, *Intelligent Design* [Downer's Grove, IL: InterVarsity Press, 1999], 20). *"In the Beginning": The Creationist Controversy*, 2-part PBS series, 1994; revised 2001; Johnson, *Darwin on Trial*, 150.

9. *"In the Beginning": The Creationist Controversy*, 2-part PBS series, 1994; revised 2001.

10. Regarding Johnson's new, expanded crusade, see Phillip E. Johnson, *Reason in the Balance: The Case against Naturalism in Science, Law & Education* (Downer's Grove, IL: InterVarsity Press, 1995).

11. William A. Dembski, *The Design Inference: Eliminating Chance through Small Probabilities* (Cambridge: Cambridge University Press, 1998), xii; this book contains Dembski's philosophical and theoretical groundwork for the intelligent-design argument, although he does not apply it much to the creation issue. I confess that this tactic of mathematical probability always reminds me of a surreal conversation I had many years ago with the author of a book purporting to demonstrate that Mikhail Gorbachev, then the leader of the Soviet Union, was the antichrist predicted in the book of Revelation. This author, who described himself as a nuclear engineer with a master's degree in theology, had calculated the odds *against* Gorbachev's being the antichrist at 710 quadrillion to one (specifically, 710,609,175,188,282,100 to 1). Balmer, *Mine Eyes Have Seen the Glory*, 205–206.

12. Dembski, *Intelligent Design*, 14. In *Creationism's Trojan Horse: The Wedge of Intelligent Design* (New York: Oxford University Press, 2004), Barbara Forrest and Paul R. Gross demonstrate that this tactic is part of a larger strategy for the intelligent-design movement. The Discovery Institute, for example, was less than enthusiastic about the court case in Dover, Pennsylvania, because it pressed the issue into local

schools (and, therefore, the courts) too soon; their strategy was first to "teach the controversy," that is, to sow doubt about evolution, and only then to proceed with curricular reforms. See Margaret Talbot, "Darwin in the Dock: Intelligent Design Has Its Day in Court," *New Yorker* (December 5, 2005): 66–77.

13. James Dao, "Sleepy Election Is Jolted by Evolution," *New York Times*, May 17, 2005, A12; Kim Kozlowski, "Evolution Battle Grows in Schools," *Detroit News*, July 24, 2005.

14. Elizabeth Bumiller, "Bush Remark Roils Debate over Teaching of Evolution," *New York Times*, August 3, 2005, A14.

15. *Kitzmiller v. Dover Area School District*, Trial transcript: Day 12 (October 19, 2005), AM session, Part 1. Behe conceded this point under cross-examination.

16. Paul Krugman, "Design for Confusion," *New York Times*, August 5, 2005, A15.

17. In the interest of full disclosure, I should reveal that while I was a doctoral student at Princeton in the early 1980s, I received a one-year graduate fellowship from the Intercollegiate Studies Institute, the Richard M. Weaver Fellowship, for the academic year 1982–1983.

18. Regarding the Baylor controversy, see Randall Balmer, "2012: A School Odyssey," *Christianity Today*, November 18, 2002, 62–69.

19. *"In the Beginning": The Creationist Controversy*, 2-part PBS series, 1994; revised 2001.

20. *"In the Beginning": The Creationist Controversy*, 2-part PBS series, 1994; revised 2001.

21. Quoted in Perry Miller and Thomas H. Johnson, eds., *The Puritans* (New York: American Book Company, 1938), 701.

22. George M. Marsden, "The Ambiguities of Academic Freedom," *Church History*, 62 (June 1993): 236.

23. In fairness to Marsden, whom I consider a friend and probably a more-or-less unwitting tool of the Religious Right, there is some evidence that he may have repented of his earlier views. In a review of D. G. Hart's *The University Gets Religion: Religious Studies in American Higher Education*, Marsden concludes that Hart's book "demonstrates that conservative Christian scholars *can* work within the norms of mainstream universities and their principle arbiters of tenure, the university presses." This is a curious statement coming from someone who also wrote that younger scholars "learn to hide their religious beliefs in professional settings" and that "the biases against speaking about Christian perspectives persist." George M. Marsden, "Christian Advocacy and the Rules of the Academic Game," in *Religious Advocacy and American History*, ed. Bruce Kuklick and D. G. Hart (Grand Rapids, MI: Wm. B. Eerdmans, 1997), 16; Marsden, *The Outrageous Idea of Christian Scholarship* (New York: Oxford University Press, 1997), 23.

24. George F. Will, "A Debate That Does Not End," *Newsweek*, July 4, 2005, 60.

CHAPTER 5

1. Constance E. Cumbey, *The Hidden Dangers of the Rainbow: The New Age Movement and Our Coming Age of Barbarism* (Shreveport, LA: Huntington House, 1983), 41; the reference to the Sierra Club appears on p. 58.

2. Cumbey, *The Hidden Dangers of the Rainbow*, 158.

3. The shooting of Texas attorney Harry Whittington by Dick Cheney during a quail hunt on February 11, 2006, was obviously not the first time in U.S. history that a sitting vice president shot someone.

4. Watt was finally forced to resign in November 1983 after he joked about the composition of an advisory group: "We have every kind of mixture you can have. I have a black. I have a woman, two Jews, and a cripple."

5. E. Calvin Beisner, *Prospects for Growth: A Biblical View of Population, Resources, and the Future* (Wheaton, IL: Crossway Books, 1990), 22, 30. Beisner also writes that "some seemingly profound ideas, like one theologically liberal denomination's protest that nuclear arms threaten all of creation, turn out to be mere imbecility" (Beisner, *Prospects for Growth*, 20).

6. Genesis 1:26 (KJV).

7. Genesis 1:21 (KJV); Psalms 145:9 (KJV). I am very much indebted to Matthew Scully's excellent book on this subject, *Dominion: The Power of Man, the Suffering of Animals, and the Call to Mercy* (New York: St. Martin's Press, 2002). Scully was a speechwriter for George W. Bush until he left the White House in August 2004.

8. Charles Colson, with Anne Morse, "Taming Beasts: Raising the Moral Status of Dogs Has Created a Breed of Snarling, Dangerous Humans," *Christianity Today*, April 2003, 120; Wesley J. Smith, "Pro-Animal or Anti-Human: A SARS Revelation," *National Review* online, April 25, 2003. Unaccountably, Colson also praises Scully's book as "excellent," a description that is even more curious because Scully criticizes his fellow conservative as "dismissive of animal rights" and notes of Colson, "On the problem of cruelty to animals, one hears only silence" (Scully, *Dominion*, 130, 131). Indeed, Scully's critique of Colson and his deafening silence on the treatment of animals extends for several pages. Colson, one suspects, didn't trouble himself to read the book before offering his encomium, which (to add further to the mystery) appears as one of the endorsements for the paperback edition of Scully's book.

9. To cite only one example, Glacier National Park in northwestern Montana had fifty glaciers when the park was established in 1910; today, only twenty remain. On the perils of global warming, see Eugene Linden, *The Winds of Change: Climate, Weather, and the Destruction of Civilizations* (New York: Simon & Schuster, 2006).

10. One of the things Bouma asks his students to do is to compute their ecological footprint by visiting a website (www.myfootprint.org). They then report their findings to the remainder of the class.

11. Matthew Scully, for instance, acknowledges that one of the reasons for the silence on the part of evangelical leaders regarding cruelty to animals "is that many ministers detect in modern environmentalism and rights talk a hint of pagan nature-worship, and avoid the subject altogether in fear of confusing the flock" (*Dominion*, 17).

12. Evangelicals may be getting their house in order on environmental issues, but they still have a way to go on grammar. *Steward*, of course (like *impact* or *network*), is not a verb.

CONCLUSION

1. Allow me to clarify that *Christianity Today* pays me for the articles I write; they do not compensate me for being on the masthead.

2. The Religious Right has tried to argue that the U.S. invasion satisfies just-war criteria. The most determined attempt to do so was crafted by Jean Bethke Elshtain and appears in the epilogue of the paperback edition of her book *Just War against Terror: The Burden of American Power in a Violent World* (New York: Basic Books, 2003). Elshtain's argument, however, conveniently ignores key pieces of evidence, including the Downing Street memorandum.

3. On the attempts to silence a NASA official who warns against global warming, see Andrew C. Revkin, "Climate Expert Says NASA Tried to Silence Him," *New York Times*, January 29, 2006. Lee R. Raymond was paid an average of $144,573 a day over the course of his thirteen-year tenure as chairman and chief executive officer of Exxon (Jad Mouawad, "For Leading Exxon to Its Riches, $144573 a Day," *New York Times*, April 15, 2006).

4. Rick Wilson, "Minimum Wage Fight on Again," CommonDreams.org, posted May 25, 2005; David Cay Johnston, "Big Gain for Rich Seen in Tax Cuts for Investments," *New York Times*, April 5, 2006. Regarding the identification of the Religious Right with the Republican Party, consider, for example, the organizations called Reformation Ohio and Ohio Restoration Project, which have actively promoted Republican candidates. See Stephanie Strom, "Group Seeks I.R.S. Inquiry of 2 Ohio Churches Accused of Improper Campaigning," *New York Times*, January 16, 2006.

5. After his Senate confirmation, Alito sent a profuse letter of thanks to James Dobson for his support.

6. To its credit, *Christianity Today* published a cover story, "Why Torture Is Always Wrong," in its February 2006 issue. A companion article, however, was rather more equivocal on the matter.

7. My request read as follows (in its entirety): "Please send me a copy of [name of organization]'s position on the Bush administration's use of torture. Thank you." I sent the request to the following Religious Right groups: Family Research Council, Vision America, Christian Coalition, Focus on the Family, Traditional Values Coalition,

American Family Association, Institute on Religion and Democracy, and the Moral Majority Coalition. The e-mail response from the Family Research Council quoted in the text was dated December 14, 2005; the response from Alan Wisdom, interim president of the Institute on Religion and Democracy, was dated January 30, 2006.

8. Regarding Arar's case, see Bob Herbert, "No Justice, No Peace," *New York Times*, February 23, 2006.

9. To their credit, some evangelical opponents of abortion are working at the grassroots level to change the moral climate around the issue. See, for example, John Leland, "Some Abortion Foes Forgo Politics," *New York Times*, January 16, 2006.

10. Patrick Henry College fund-raising letter dated November 30, 2005; Family Research Council fund-raising letter dated January 2006; regarding Parsley, see "Brownback's Team," *Rolling Stone*, February 9, 2006, 53.

11. The reference to "the least of these" appears in Matthew 25:40.

12. Micah 6:8b (TNIV); Zechariah 7:9–10 (TNIV).

13. Matthew 5:9 (TNIV); Matthew 25:42–43 (TNIV). Regarding the lack of distinction among races and between the sexes, see Galatians 2:28.

14. Quoted in Rosemary Radford Ruether and Rosemary Skinner Keller, eds, *The Nineteenth Century*, vol. 1 of *Women and Religion in America: A Documentary History* (New York: Harper & Row, 1981), 211. Historically, it is true that the churches bore much of the responsibility for social welfare until the early decades of the twentieth century. With the onset of the Great Depression, however, the social problems were so overwhelming and their causes so systemic that the government stepped in to relieve the burden. So far, at least, I haven't seen much inclination on the part of the churches to reclaim their earlier responsibilities. (The faith-based initiative programs use taxpayer money for their activities.)

15. Jack Newfield, "Ralph Reed's Gamble," *The Nation* (July 12, 2004); Peter Stone, "Ralph Reed's Other Cheek," *Mother Jones* (November/December 2004). On Reed's ambitions, see Ralph Z. Hallow, "Reed Said to See Georgia as Path to White House," *Washington Times*, January 18, 2005. The precipitous fall of a power broker like Jack Abramoff, who is an observant Jew, might well give pause to members of the Jewish political right who have thrown their lot in with Religious Right extremists.

16. Regarding Perkins, see Appendix.

17. Matthew 7:3 and 23:16 (TNIV).

18. 1 Corinthians 15:33 (TNIV); Matthew 16:26 (TNIV).

19. Quoted in John F. Wilson and Donald L. Drakeman, eds., *Church and State in America History: Key Documents, Decisions, and Commentary from the Past Three Centuries*, 3rd ed. (Boulder, CO: Westview Press, 2003), 87.

20. Matthew 22:21 (TNIV).

21. Colossians 2:15 (KJV).

22. Matthew 6:19 (TNIV).

APPENDIX

1. See, for example, Mark Silk, *Spiritual Politics: Religion and America since World War II* (New York: Simon & Schuster, 1988), ch. 2. The configuration of the Temple of Religion at the World's Fair of 1939–1940 illustrates the exclusionary nature of this new Judeo-Christian alliance. The fair's organizers clearly intended to celebrate Protestantism, Catholicism, and Judaism, and they systematically rejected proposals from religious groups that, in their judgment, fell outside the pale of respectability. See Jesse T. Todd, "Imagining the Future of American Religion at the New York World's Fair, 1939–40" (Ph.D. dissertation, Columbia University, 1996).

2. Roy Moore and other "originalists," as I noted in chapter 2, argue that the only religious expressions guaranteed by the First Amendment are Christianity and Judaism—and Moore includes the latter only in his more expansive moments. Regarding the latter point, that Jews don't lie awake at night worrying about the public posting of the Ten Commandments, when I mentioned that in the course of a panel discussion at the Ninety-second Street Y in New York City recently, a rabbi on the panel shot back, "Yes, we do!"—meaning that Jews do worry about posting the Decalogue, and they don't want it.

3. For further analysis of this conspiracy theory, see Didi Herman, *The Anti-Gay Agenda: Orthodox Vision and the Christian Right* (Chicago: University of Chicago Press, 1997), chs. 2–3; Ralph Reed, *Active Faith: How Christians Are Changing the Soul of American Politics* (New York: Free Press, 1996), 264; James Dobson, "Setting the Record Straight," *Dr. Dobson's Newsletter* (February 2005).

4. Once again, the Religious Right is inconsistent on this point, asserting the principle of states' rights on some matters, but, at the same time, seeking a federal amendment to outlaw civil unions and same-sex marriages.

5. Max Blumenthal, "Justice Sunday Preachers," *The Nation* (online), April 26, 2005.

6. Reed, *Active Faith*, 5.

7. Family Research Council fund-raising letter dated January 2006. Italics in original.

Index